EXPERT PAINT:

PAINTING KITCHENS

EXPERT PAINT:
PAINTING KITCHENS

QUARRY BOOKS

How to Choose and Use the Right Paint for Your Kitchen Walls, Ceilings, Floors, Cabinets, Countertops, and Appliances

Steve Jordan | Judy Ostrow

First published in the United States of America by
Quarry Books, an imprint of
Rockport Publishers, Inc.
33 Commercial Street
Gloucester, Massachusetts 01930-5089
Telephone: (978) 282-9590
Fax: (978) 283-2742
www.rockpub.com

Library of Congress Cataloging-in-Publication Data
Jordan, Steve, [date]
    Expert paint : painting kitchens : how to choose and use the right paint for
your kitchen walls, ceilings, floors, cabinets, countertops, and appliances /
Steve Jordan and Judy Ostrow.
        p.   cm.
    ISBN 1-59253-098-2 (pbk.)
    1. House painting. 2. Interior decoration. 3. Kitchens. I. Ostrow, Judy.
II. Title.
TT323.J69 2004
698'.14–dc22
                                                                                2004011038
                                                                                        CIP

ISBN 1-59253-098-2
10 9 8 7 6 5 4 3 2 1

Cover Design: Bob's Your Uncle
Design: Roycroft Design (www.roycroftdesign.com)
Cover Image: Courtesy of Crown Point Cabinetry (www.crown-point.com)
                        main image; Courtesy of ICI Paints (www.ici.com) bottom row
Back Cover Images:Courtesy of ICI Paints (www.ici.com)
Illustrations: Lorraine Dey, Dey Studios

Printed in Singapore

CONTENTS

INTRODUCTION

Why buy this book?

You might be curious—why a book about painting kitchens? Why not a book about painting kitchens, bathrooms, living rooms, the whole shebang? If you live like most of us, kitchens are one of the two hardest-used rooms in your house. (The other is the bathroom.) Kitchens are no longer just the domain of the cook and bottle washer but a favorite gathering place of family and friends, thus they are more frequently redecorated than any other room. Visit most kitchens in America, and you'll find that they have been painted two to four times more often than the other rooms in the house. Kitchens also present painting and decorating challenges not found in other areas; considering special cleaning needs, choosing the appropriate paint for adhesion, and making the paint blend with cabinet finishes, floors, countertops, and appliances are all part of the pie. If you can paint your kitchen, you can paint anything, so let's go.

Section 1, Preparation, Painting, and Special Projects, covers the tools, materials, and techniques necessary to get started and to complete a successful painting project. You'll learn how the professionals do it and get tips to make difficult tasks easier. Because choosing an appropriate type of paint can be confusing, we explain exactly what you need for your kitchen so that you can approach a paint salesperson with confidence and ease.

Section 2, Palettes and Inspiration, discusses style and color. You'll find a wide variety of palette ideas that can visually transform a space. The palettes range from traditional favorites to trendy, eye-catching combinations. You'll also see how color can work to enhance the function and feeling of this important room.

OPPOSITE Kitchens are the hardest-working room in the house, and require durable, washable paint surfaces that can stand up to grease, smoke, and food stains. When choosing paint, purchase a quality brand with a finish that has long-lasting potential.

LEFT With a little imagination and a few tools, paint delivers more dramatic results than any other decorating material. Semigloss or high-gloss finishes are the right choice for kitchens, where easy cleanup is essential for the life of painted surfaces.

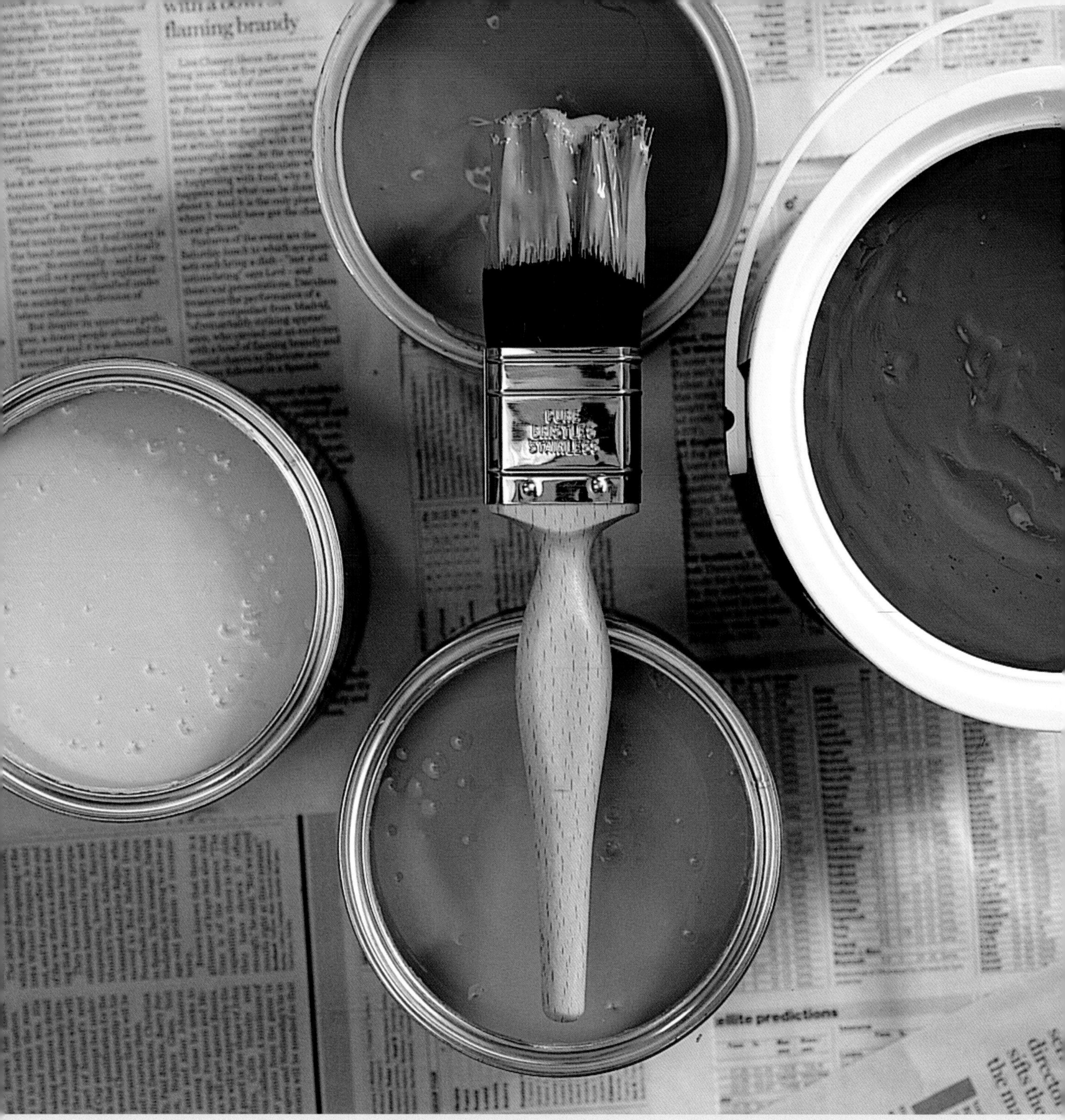

SECTION 01 PREPARATION, PAINTING, AND SPECIAL PROJECTS

Chapter I: Tools and Materials

The Big Cover-up

Painting is a popular do-it-yourself project: it doesn't require expensive materials and tools to create a great-looking job, and many of the materials and tools can be thrown away at the end of the project. On the other hand, if you enjoy painting and know that this project is one of many in the future, splurge; purchase quality tools and materials that will last for many jobs, create a neater appearance with ease, save time, and—in the long run—save money.

Cloth Drop Cloths

Professional painters cover floors with canvas drop cloths. These cloths are usually made of cotton, but butyl- or rubber-backed cloths are also common. Cotton drop cloths come in a variety of weights, such as medium, heavy duty, and extra heavy duty. The heavier the cloth, the better it protects the floors and the longer it lasts. The rating is sometimes expressed in ounce weight. Purchase 10- or 12-ounce cloths for paint protection and lighter 8-ounce cloths for protecting the floors from foot traffic in the area where the work takes place. When you take care of them, cotton drop cloths last a lifetime and can be cleaned in a washing machine. Rubber-backed cloths are usually less expensive and offer excellent drip protection, but they do not last as long as cotton cloths.

Drop cloths come in various sizes. Runners are typically 4 feet (1.2 m) wide and 12 or 15 feet (3.7 or 4.6 m) long. Use runners to cover the floors from the exterior door to the work area or to cover narrow areas behind furniture. Larger cloths, 9-by-12 square feet (2.7 by 3.7 sq. m) or 12-by-15 square feet (3.7 by 4.6 sq. m), are usually available as well. Fastidious painters and finicky homeowners do not like dusty or soiled cloths used on clean or new floors. To avoid this mess, mark one side of your new drop cloth with a large spray-painted X. Always place the X side facedown; that way, it remains cleaner than if both sides are reversed frequently.

LEFT A heavy-duty cotton drop cloth is a sound investment for homeowners and professionals. The protection it provides will prevent damage from drips and accidental spills as well as wear and tear from foot traffic in the work area.

Plastic Drop Cloths

For one-time-only use, you can't beat plastic (polyethylene) drop cloths, used alone or to supplement cloth drop cloths. Plastic drop cloths are sold in room sizes and by the roll. Your first consideration should be the mil thickness of the plastic. Use 1-mil plastic or thinner (sometimes called painter's plastic) to cover furniture, curtains, or wall coverings, but don't try to walk on it because it's too thin. Use 2- or 3-mil plastic on floors for a short-duration job and 4-mil plastic for a job extended over a long period of time. Multipurpose polyurethane tarps, typically used to cover firewood and boats, are also good for covering floors. For covering small areas, room-size plastic drops should suit your needs. For larger cover-ups, buy a 100- to 400-foot (30.5 to 121.9 m) roll of plastic at a good paint store or home improvement center—it is far less expensive than buying individual pieces. If you are willing to pay the price, pretaped plastic drop cloths combine tape and plastic to ease the task of draping walls and furniture.

Plastic is impervious to paint, but it is difficult to walk on and tends to "creep" away from areas you want to protect. Prevent this creep by taping the plastic cloths to the floor at the baseboard.

Don't try to reuse plastic tarps and drops cloths for interior painting. The dry drips, splatters, and spills frequently loosen from the plastic and fall onto floors and furniture creating a mess that is indistinguishable from wet drips, making your final cleanup difficult.

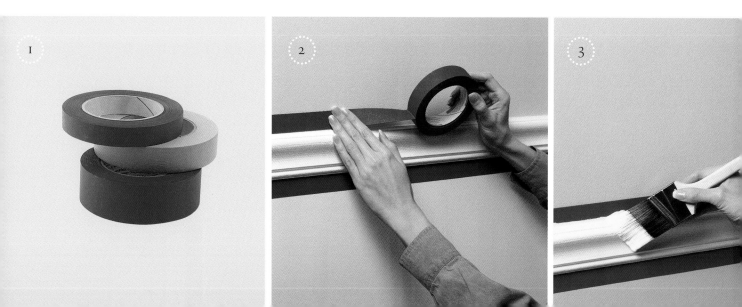

Masking Tape and Paper

The hand masker is one of the handiest gadgets ever invented. It allows you to mask up to 60 linear yards (54.9 m) of floor, railings, windows, or whatever with the tape of your choice and paint-resistant paper. This inexpensive tool is a must-have for avid do-it-yourselfers. You can use a hand masker to provide excellent protection of hardwood or carpeted floors, light fixtures, trim, wall coverings, and appliances. Purchase the paper in widths of 3 to 12 inches (7.5 to 30.5 cm) to suit the job, and choose the masking tape according to the duration of the job and the material over which you are taping. Proprietary tape-and-paper products such as Easy Mask combine a roll of brown paper with a sticky edge for precise masking needs.

Masking tape manufacturers have responded to the difficulty related to using old-fashioned, general-purpose masking tape when painting—if it remained on a surface too long, it wouldn't come off, and it frequently ruined delicate surfaces such as wallpaper. Improved safe-release masking tapes are guaranteed to be easily removable for a specified time (usually 10 or 14 days) from all surfaces, including the sensitive ones. These tapes are pricey but worth it. When purchasing tape, ask your paint or home improvement center specialist which is best for your job. You may encounter situations when combining tapes is useful. For example, when securing plastic cloth drops at the baseboard to cover a floor, lay safe-release tape on the floor and join the plastic to the safe-release tape with general-purpose masking tape for a trouble-free seal.

ABOVE Masking off hardware, appliances, countertops, and floors protected the variety of surfaces in this hardworking kitchen. This good preparation allows the painter to apply paint treatments effectively and makes the final cleanup easier.

Tips

MASKING TAPE AND PAINTER'S TAPE ARE MANUFACTURED FOR VARIOUS TASKS.

#1 Safe–release painter's tape is ideal for use over freshly dried paint.

#2 After applying a strip of masking tape, go over the tape again, pressing the edges firmly with your fingertips. This adheres the tape to the surface and prevents paint from seeping underneath.

#3 To remove masking tape after painting, wait until the paint is dry. Then slowly peel the tape off at a 90 degree angle to minimize tearing.

Hand Tools

You may already own many of the hand tools needed to complete a successful paint job. A list of the most common tools and description of their uses follows.

SCREWDRIVERS— SLOTTED AND PHILLIPS

Screwdrivers are used to remove switch and receptacle plates, hardware, HVAC registers, and curtain brackets. In most cases, a battery-operated screwdriver or drill makes removal quicker, but a manual screwdriver is often necessary. A slotted screwdriver is also useful for opening paint cans.

PUTTY AND SPACKLING KNIVES

A flexible 1½-inch (3.8 cm) putty knife is indispensable for filling nail holes and hairline cracks. Use 4- to 6-inch (10.2 to 15.2 cm) spackling knives, also called joint or taping knives, to apply spackling compound, drywall compound, and fillers. A five-in-one tool serves as a scraper and putty knife and also has a curved face for raking paint from roller covers.

PAINT CAN OPENER

Although a slotted screwdriver can open a new can of paint easily, it takes a paint can opener to unseal a paint-encrusted top without ruining the lid.

CAULKING GUN

Use a caulking gun to apply caulk from a tube. Avoid the least expensive guns; look for a dripless model, which usually costs about 10 dollars.

STIRRING STICKS

You should get stirring sticks free with the purchase of a can of paint; expect at least one for each color. Although your paint should be well shaken at the store, use stirring sticks to rake dregs from the bottom of the can, to stir in water or paint thinner, and to rake excess paint from your roller cover at the end of the job.

DUSTER BRUSH

Use a duster brush to remove dust and debris from corners, especially around window muntins and raised-panel doors. You can buy a special duster brush, but most old, worn paintbrushes serve the purpose. After you use a paintbrush as a duster, don't use it for painting.

SPINNER

A painter's spinner cleans and spins excess water or solvent from brushes and rollers. This tool is not a must-have, but anyone who paints often and likes to clean their tools well should have one.

LADDER

Every household should have a safe, steady ladder for changing lightbulbs and painting. Don't purchase a ladder that is too short or too tall. A 4-, 5-, or 6-foot (1.2, 1.5, or 1.8m) ladder is adequate for working in a house with 8-foot (2.4 m) ceilings. Ladders are rated for safety and weight. Type III ladders, designed for occasional use by homeowners, are the lightest, with a 200-pound (90.7 kg) load limit. Type II commercial ladders are sturdier and designed for loads up to 225 pounds (102.1 kg). Type III and Type III heavy duty are industrial quality and rated for loads up to 250 pounds (113.4 kg). Note that some ladders have folding platforms for your tools, whereas others omit the platform and provide holes in the top for hammers and other tools. The folding platform is handy for holding a paint bucket. If your ladder does not have a platform, use a bucket hook (also called a pot hook) to attach the bucket to the ladder rungs. Do not hold the bucket in one hand and paint with the other; use the ladder platform or hook for your bucket.

POWER TOOLS

Power tools are seldom necessary for most small painting projects, but they can speed up the work. A finish sander (also called a pad sander) is commonly used for sanding cabinets, doors, and long, flat expanses of trim. In some cases, a more aggressive random-orbit sander can be more efficient than a finish sander. Do not use an orbital or drill-attached rotary sander; this tool mars your work with unsightly swirls. Use a heat gun to remove thick, uneven, or cratered layers of paint, such as is frequently found on windowsills. Finally, how can anyone do anything without an electric or cordless drill at hand?

Specialty Preparation Tools

Some paint jobs require specialized tools. A description of some of these tools follows.

WALLPAPER SCORERS, SCRAPERS, AND SPRAYERS

The secret of removing old wallpaper is often discovered after you begin. A handheld spray bottle is all you need for most jobs, but a hand-pump yard sprayer comes in handy for larger jobs. When warm water or steam does not penetrate the surface adequately to dampen underlying glue, use a wallpaper-scoring tool to puncture the paper's surface with thousands of tiny holes. You can usually rent sprayers and scorers from a paint store for a modest fee. Zinsser manufacturers a good scoring tool called PAPERTIGER. Rent a wallpaper steamer at your paint store or rental center. Steamers are seldom necessary except for the most stubborn removal projects.

When the wallpaper is sufficiently softened, use a stiff, sharp scraper to remove the paper and glue. Most scrapers work well enough, but you can purchase specialized wallpaper scrapers at your paint store. You'll also need a scrubbing pad or a sponge with an attached scrubbing pad to remove the remaining glue.

Materials for Preparation

Professional painters always caution that a good paint job depends on *preparation, preparation, preparation.* Fortunately, the required preparatory materials are few and inexpensive.

SANDPAPER

Use sandpaper to roughen old glossy paint, smooth sags and runs, and remove dust and other particles between coats. General-purpose, aluminum-oxide sandpaper comes in convenient 9-by-11-inch (22.9 by 27.9 cm) sheets that can be divided in smaller pieces. Grit size denotes the roughness of the paper. For example, 80-grit sandpaper is typically the roughest used on an interior paint job—usually for removing sags and smoothing uneven or chipped surfaces. A 220-grit sandpaper has a fine texture and is usually adequate for final finishing. Extra fine 320-grit or higher is used for a final sanding under high-gloss finishes, in brightly lit areas, or on furniture. Sandpaper weight is rated by an A or C. The A weight paper is thin and flimsy but adequate for most jobs. The C weight paper is heavier, holds up to hard sanding, and is the preferred sandpaper for use with power sanders.

Wet-or-dry sandpaper, an automotive finishing product, is more expensive than ordinary sandpaper. As the name indicates, you can use it dry, like ordinary sandpaper, or dipped in water or oil for a finer finish. When dipped in water, wet-or-dry sandpaper is ideal for smoothing existing latex paint that can clog ordinary sandpaper. A 200-grit wet-or-dry sandpaper is excellent for removing runs, sags, and heavy brush marks. Use 320-grit wet-or-dry sandpaper for smoothing out the surface before applying a final coat of finish. You can also use wet-or-dry sandpaper dipped in water for sanding lead-based paint to avoid releasing lead dust all over the room.

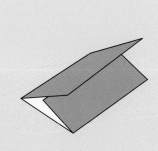

Tips

HOW TO FOLD SANDPAPER

When you sand with sheets of sandpaper, folding the paper correctly makes the job easier and the paper last longer. For sanding large areas, first fold the paper in half. Then, using a putty knife, rip the paper cleanly at the crease into two rectangular pieces. For smaller areas, fold the sheet into fourths (one fold in each direction). Holding the sand side down, fold each piece into thirds with one usable side enclosed and two usable sides exposed. When the two outer surfaces are worn out, refold the sheet and use the remaining sanded surface.

SANDING SPONGES

Sanding sponges are useful tools for sanding curved surfaces because they conform to the shape of the surface. In addition, the sponge on the back protects your fingers. These sponges are available in fine, medium, and course grits and can be used dry or dipped in water.

STEEL WOOL

Use steel wool for stripping paint and polishing brass—that's about all. Steel wool is a great product for some chores, but I've never found much use for it in painting. The tiny strands break, hide in cracks, and reappear to mar the painted surface. They burrow in your fingers as steel splinters, and they can rust under water-based finishes.

FILLERS

Far too many fillers, spackling compounds, and patching compounds are available to mention them all individually. Available in pints, quarts, and gallons, spackling compounds are great for filling nail holes, dings, and minor wall cracks. Spackling compound comes in two types—ordinary and lightweight. Everyone has a favorite; I prefer the ordinary type, which dries more slowly than the lightweight variety but provides a dense, hard fill. Despite manufacturers' claims, two or more coats are usually necessary to achieve a smooth finish. Many carpenters prefer the one-step hole-fill technique of applying a large amount over each hole, allowing it to dry, and then sanding the filler with a power sander. This method works, but it makes a lot of dust.

JOINT COMPOUND

Joint compound, also called "mud", is available premixed in quarts, gallons, five gallons, and in powder form. Use this product for more serious repairs, such as extensive cracks, leveling large areas of walls or ceilings, and repairing plaster. Note that you can sand some varieties more easily than others. When a lot of filling or repair work must be done, joint compound is far more economical than spackling compound. Joint compound is also far less expensive when purchased by the five-gallon bucket; you can always discard the remainder or give it to a neighbor.

OTHER FILLERS

Plaster is best applied by professionals and is generally available only at masonry supply stores. Automotive polyester body filler (such as Bondo) is useful for quick, deep, and shallow trim repairs where you want to fill, sand, and paint all in one day (or maybe all in one hour). This material is difficult to sand and has a strong solvent odor.

ABOVE Sanding sponges conform to contours and protect your hands. They can also be dipped in water to achieve an ultrasmooth finish.

CAULK

Sold in 10-ounce (283.5 g) tubes, caulk has aesthetic and utilitarian uses. It fills unsightly cracks or gaps between trim and walls, between pieces of over-lapped trim, and in cracks in corners. It also prevents air infiltration through the walls. Make sure to use paintable caulk—100 percent silicone caulk is not paintable. Also avoid inexpensive painter's caulk. Look for siliconized acrylic caulk or acrylic caulk with silicone, both of which can be painted. High-qual-ity caulks have a 30- or 40-year limited warranty, are easy to apply, and clean up with water. When the need for caulking is minimal—say, for a few hair-line cracks—purchase a 5-ounce (141.7 g) squeeze tube of white acrylic tub-and-tile caulk and forget about a caulking gun. Tub-and-tile caulk is also easier to use in tight, cramped areas where the gun does not fit.

Tips

HOW TO APPLY CAULK

How you apply caulk often makes the difference between a fair-looking job and a great-looking job. Here's how to do it: With a sharp razor knife, cut the end off the caulk tube's plastic nozzle at an angle, leaving a hole, about $1/8$ inch (0.3 cm) across. At this point, some tubes are ready to use; others have a membrane inside the spout that must be punctured with wire. Next, put the tip of the tube over the crack. While pulling the trigger slowly and evenly, pull the tip along the crack with the sharp part of the tip compressing the caulk into the crack. When you have completed 12 inches (30.5 cm), or maybe 6 feet (1.8 m), wrap a damp rag around your forefinger and remove the excess caulk. The goal is to fill the crack without removing too much caulking and to remove all caulk around the crack. When applying caulk in right angles, such as the junction of a wall and trim, avoid rounding out the corner by leaving too much caulk. Caulking guns are notorious for dripping—even the dripless models. Always lay the gun on a piece of newspaper or cardboard when you are not using it.

RAGS

You'll seldom find a painter without a rag, and it's usually a 100 percent cotton rag. Old T-shirts make the best rags, with high-quality, lint-free paper rags (such as Scott Rags-in-a-Box) a close second. Avoid synthetic rags, which are not sufficiently absorbent. Paper towels leave lint on the surface, and old clothing with buttons, zippers, or brads can scratch a delicate surface.

Application Tools

BRUSHES

A quality brush appropriate for the project at hand is a joy. Most people who complain that they hate to paint have never used a good brush. Achieving an acceptable job with a two-dollar brush is impossible and frustrating. Typical paintbrushes for interior painting are $1\frac{1}{2}$ to 3 inches (3.8 to 7.6 cm) wide; smaller and larger brushes are available, but it is unusual to need them. Use $1\frac{1}{2}$ to $2\frac{1}{2}$ inch (3.8 to 6.4 cm) sash brushes for trim. The angular sash brush is the most popular choice for small or delicate trim work because it allows you to work into tight corners. For "cutting in" around trim and into wall and ceiling corners, use a $2\frac{1}{2}$ to 3 inch (6.4 to 7.6 cm) wall brush. These brushes hold more paint than sash brushes, enabling you to work more quickly. When choosing a brush, you usually can't go wrong buying a professional brush, such as those manufactured by Purdy, Wooster, Corona, Bestt Liebco, PPG, Prager, or Sherwin-Williams.

Selection of a quality brush can be confusing, so let's begin by lumping them into two categories. Pure Chinese bristle brushes are made from the bristles of unique Chinese hogs and are superior for use in *oil paint* only. If you use them with water-based latex paint—even for a short time—they swell and become uselessly limp, ruined forever. Notice that some brush bristles are black and others are off-white. White bristles are bleached and are best used for oil-based varnishes. They also work well with paint, but they wear out more quickly than the black bristles. The finest bristle brushes, used for clear finishing and exceptional painted finishes, are a blend of ox hair and select hog bristle. As you might expect, these brushes are very expensive and are used by discriminating painters.

Use synthetic-bristle brushes for water-based paint and oil paint. These brushes are typically nylon, nylon-polyester blends, and proprietary blends, such as Chinex by Dupont or the pure bristle and nylon blend by Wooster.

Quality brushes have two features that are easy to overlook. The first is tapered bristles (also called chiseled). The ends of the bristles should taper into a wedge to allow you to work into tight spaces. The second feature is flagged bristle tips, meaning that the end of the bristles divide into several smaller bristles—similar to split ends in your hair. The metal band between the bristles and the handle, the ferrule, should be stainless steel or rust resistant. Whether the handle is unfinished, painted, varnished, or synthetic has little to do with the quality of the brush; most quality brushes have unfinished handles. Loose bristles are the sign of a poor quality brush. Bristles should be firmly set and have a good spring when raked across your palm.

Disposable foam or bristle brushes (sometimes called chip brushes) are handy for applying sealers over small stains and for touch-up work.

ABOVE A quality brush is a joy to use and will last many years if cared for properly. Use brushes with Chinese bristles for oil-based paints and synthetic bristles for water-based paints.

Cleaning Brushes

Cleaning brushes is everyone's least favorite part of the job. That's why so many cheap brushes are purchased —so they can be tossed at the end of the day. Although there are no quick fixes for brush cleaning, a few helpful hints can make it easer.

BRUSHES USED IN LATEX PAINT

Brushes used in latex paint can either be cleaned at the end of the day or tightly wrapped in plastic and stored in the refrigerator for a day or two. When leaving the job for a half-hour or more, wrap the bristles in plastic (sandwich bags are excellent for this) or foil to keep them from drying out. To clean your brush, first rinse off the excess paint in the sink. Use a wire brush to remove any paint dried on the outer bristles. Continue washing the brush by bending the bristles in your palm to remove paint from the tips to the ferrule. Use a dab of dishwashing detergent for the final rinse. At this point, the water squeezed from the bristles should be as clean as drinking water. To store your brush, remove excess water by spinning the brush between your palms, lightly kicking the ferrule against the toe of your shoe, or using a painter's spinner. Return the brush to its original cardboard holder, or fold paper around the bristles to re-form and protect the bristles.

BRUSHES USED IN OIL PAINT

Cleaning oil-based paint from brushes at the end of the day takes a long time and a lot of solvent—so don't do it. If you are using the brush the next day, wipe excess paint from the ferrule, wrap the brush tightly in plastic, and store it in the freezer. If you are finished with the brush, why not let the brush partially clean itself? Use a razor knife to make a slit in the plastic lid of a coffee can just long enough to insert the brush handle. Pour enough mineral spirits* into the can so that the bristles are fully immersed. Next, insert the brush handle into the lid slit, adjusting it so the bristles are in the mineral spirits but not touching the bottom of the can when the lid is replaced. After a few hours or a day or two, most of the excess paint drops to the bottom of the can, making it much easier to clean the brush. You can also use a spring clamp and a canning jar for this method. Mineral spirits squeezed out of the bristles for the final rinse should be a clear as possible—somewhere between skim milk and clean water. Cover the dirty mineral spirits and set it aside for a few days. The paint settles to the bottom of the container, and the clear solvent at the top can be reused for thinning paint or cleaning brushes.

*Mineral Spirits (sometimes referred to as "paint thinner") is a petroleum based solvent used to reduce (thin) and clean up oil-based and alkyd paints, varnish, and enamels. Mineral spirits largely replaced turpentine and is less toxic than turpentine. Low odor mineral spirits is less fragrant than ordinary mineral spirits. Mineral spirits is also good for cleaning black heel marks off tile or laminate floors; for cleaning adhesive stickers off glass or china; removing masking tape residue, and for removing road tar from automobiles.

ROLLER COVERS

Roller covers are available in 7 and 9 inch (17.8 and 22.9 cm) lengths for rolling walls or other flat items such as slab doors or cabinet shelves. Select a roller cover suitable for surface you are painting. Nap covers of $^1/_4$ inch and $^3/_8$ inch (0.6 cm and 1 cm) are best for smooth surfaces; use $^1/_2$ and $^3/_4$-inch (1.3 and 1.9 cm) nap covers for textured or rough walls. The recommended use is always expressed on the packaging. Do not use cheap, disposable roller covers because they frequently shed fibers into the paint and ruin the finish.

For special projects like painting cabinets, flat trim, or behind toilet tanks and radiators, mini-rollers are handy and speed up the process. Covers for mini-rollers are similar to larger covers and are also available in foam.

ABOVE A miniroller speeds up painting and reaches deep into cabinets. These handy tools are also good for painting behind toilet bowls, radiators, and heavy appliances.

RIGHT Use roller covers in 7 and 9 inch (17.8 and 22.9 cm) lengths for painting walls and ceilings. Minirollers are great for hard-to-reach areas, cabinets, and doors.

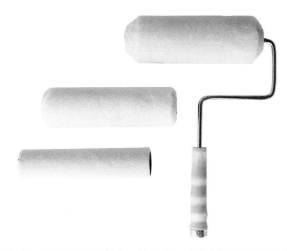

Cleaning Roller Covers

Painters frequently debate whether it's better to clean roller covers or just throw them away. Two things are certain: it takes a long time to clean a roller cover saturated in latex paint, and it's never worth your time to clean a roller used in oil-based paint. If you want to discard the cover, don't feel bad about it. Just wrap a plastic grocery bag around the wet cover, pull it off into the garbage, and then clean the frame.

Ah, but for the frugal and for jobs requiring multiple covers used in latex paint, the following methods can simplify the cleaning process. First, rake excess paint from the cover using a paint stick or a five-in-one tool*. Next, pour enough clean water into a bucket to cover the roller cover. Drop the cover into the water and let it soak for a day, or even a week. At this point, most of the paint will have dropped to the bottom of the bucket and cleaning will be easier. Remove the remaining paint in a laundry sink or with a garden hose. Spin out the remaining water with a painter's spinner or by reinserting the cover on the frame and rolling it rapidly over a board. The water removed during the final rinse should be clear.

*Five-in-one tool: A five-in-one tool is the combination of a paint scraper, window putty remover, spackling knife, gouger, and paint roller clearner—basically a redesign of the putty knife.

ROLLER FRAMES

The roller frame holds the roller cover. The frame should be sturdy to prevent its arm from bending. The handle should have an opening for screwing an extension pole to the frame.

ROLLER PANS AND BUCKETS

A roller pan holds paint in a convenient pool, leaving space at the top of the pan for working the paint evenly into the roller. Large professional-size pans hold more paint and are sturdier than inexpensive pans. Most paint stores sell inexpensive plastic liners that fit these pans and allow you to switch colors in the middle of a job while using the same pan. You can usually use the inserts several times. For larger jobs, painters frequently use an inexpensive wire grid inserted into a five-gallon bucket. Large roller buckets with built-in grids for convenience are also available. Buckets are easier to move around the room than pans and harder to inadvertently step in or tip over.

PAINT PADS

Paint pads are do-it-yourself tools designed to neatly cut around trim and ceilings and to access hard-to-reach areas. You may find paint pads useful, but they do not completely take the place of a brush.

ABOVE Paint pads take over where skill disappears. They are also great for creating straight lines between wall and ceiling paints.

SPRAYERS

Advertisements for sprayers state that these tools significantly speed up painting; they can also create messy overspray that is difficult or impossible to remove as well as uneven accumulations of paint, and they are potentially dangerous.

Airless Sprayers

Airless sprayers and airless-assisted rollers are appropriate for some new construction work but not for small projects or novice painters. They are best used on large expanses of walls, ceilings, and trim. A puncture wound from an airless sprayer is very serious and can be deadly. Use these tools only with the guidance of a professional painter.

HVLP Sprayers

HVLP sprayers (high-volume, low-pressure) are used for trim work and cabinets because they provide a smooth, even surface and a minimum of overspray. Most inexpensive HVLP sprayers are very slow, and spraying thick materials requires excessive thinning. As with airless sprayers, seek professional guidance when using this tool or get plenty of practice on scrap wood or cardboard before beginning your project.

Conventional Spray Equipment

Conventional spray equipment has been used for architectural and automotive painting for nearly 100 years. This equipment is not appropriate for residential spraying unless used for small items, such as register covers or small, ornate trim details. The excessive overspray produced by this equipment creates a mess and sometimes a blinding fog.

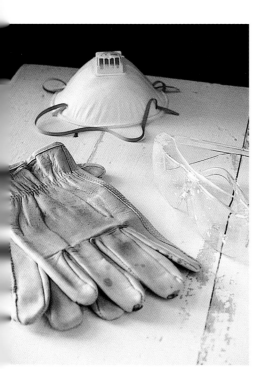

ABOVE The three most important personal safety tools are gloves, a respirator or dust mask, and eye protection.

When using any type of sprayer, provide plenty of ventilation and wear a NIOSH/MSHA(National Institute for Occupational Safety and Health/Mine Safety and Health Administration)–approved respirator to prevent inhalation of the paint. Light paper-particle masks are not sufficient protection. Protect your hair, face, arms, and all exposed parts of your body from the paint. If the product is flammable, extinguish all pilot lights and sources of fire to prevent a catastrophic explosion.

(See page 123 for resources.)

Safety Issues

Painting can be fun, but it is always important to heed all safety precautions related to the tools or materials you are using.

- Chemicals and noxious paints require adequate ventilation. Products that have never bothered you before might make you sick in an enclosed area; they might make a chemical-sensitive person extremely ill. Some extremely flammable products require that all pilot lights be turned off, so read label directions and precautions carefully.

- Maintain all safety devices, guards, and protective covers on your tools, and ensure that grounding plugs are intact.

- Many old construction materials contain asbestos or lead. If demolition is part of your project, materials should be tested and, if necessary, abatement procedures undertaken by a qualified professional.

- If lead paint is present, children and pregnant women must not work or play in the area. If lead paint is sanded, scraped, or removed, it must be done using the correct procedures. Most county health departments and many paint stores provide free brochures describing these procedures and the dangers of lead poisoning.

- If you are living in a construction site, keep your living area clean of construction debris and dust. Don't bring in lead dust and asbestos fibers. Change out of your work clothes before entering your living space.

- Keep your work site clean of construction debris that could cause accidents.

- Finally, if you're tired, put your tools away and do something else.

Selecting Paint

BUY A QUALITY PRODUCT

Always purchase the best paint you can afford; there is no economy in buying cheap paint. Ideally, paint should cover the old surface or color adequately, resist sags and runs when applied correctly, and hold up to the rigors it was designed for—wear, scrubbing, fading, chipping, and so on. Manufacturers usually sell several qualities of paint; buying the top-of-the-line offering of any major manufacturer is a safe bet that you've made a good purchase. Although manufacturer claims of "one-coat coverage" and "20-year guarantee" are encouraging, don't assume they are true, even for the best paints. Painters almost always apply more than one coat, and guarantees are extremely limited.

If you plan to paint unusual surfaces—metals, laminates, glass, and so on— ask your paint salesperson if you can review the manufacturer's specification manual for architectural coatings. You'll find recommendations and specifications for the manufacturer's full line of coatings, both common and specialized.

VISITING PAINT STORES AND HOME CENTERS

Your local paint and decorating store is the best place to purchase paint and get advice. To get the correct product and sound advice, choose a retailer that specializes in selling paint to retail customers and professional painters. Arrive at the paint store with as much information as possible about your project to help the salesperson assist you. For example, know if you are paint-ing new materials, preprimed materials, over old paint or varnish, or over stains. If repainting old paint, it helps to know what kind of paint was used— latex, oil, or varnish.

Determining the Type of Existing Paint and Why

Knowing the type of paint that was last used on a surface goes a long way toward ensuring a successful, enduring paint job. Some old surfaces are tricky to paint, and adhesion between the new and old layers takes special preparation. Oil-based paints stick best to oil-based paints, and water-based (latex) paints stick best to water-based paints. When applying new latex paint over old latex paint and new oil-based paint over old oil-based paint, preparation of the old surface is relatively easy. But when you want to apply latex paint over oil-based paint, preparation of the old surface is crucial. The best method to determine the type of paint you have is to lightly wipe the surface with a rag soaked in denatured alcohol. If the alcohol melts the surface, the old paint is water based. If the alcohol has little effect on the old paint, it's oil based.

ABOVE Both latex and oil-based paint can provide an attractive, durable finish. Knowing which kind of paint you are covering is important in choosing your new paint.

WHICH IS BEST, LATEX OR OIL?

Latex

Latex is the most commonly sold paint today. The word *latex* is a misnomer, a holdover from the early water-based formulas of the 1940s and 1950s. Latex has remained in today's lexicon to include most of the architectural coatings that are reducible and clean up with water; the correct term, however, is water borne. Most interior latex paints are vinyl-acrylic mixtures or 100 percent acrylic formulas. One hundred percent acrylic paints are usually top quality, lasting longer and resisting fading longer than the vinyl-acrylic mixtures.

The old painter's saying, nothing sticks to latex like latex, sums up the reason for applying latex paint over older latex paint—adhesion of the new to the old is excellent. Also, latex paints are formulated to remain flexible for the life of the coating, so it's a bad idea to cover an existing latex paint with an oil-based paint that soon becomes hard and brittle.

Oil based

Forced by government regulation to reduce air pollution, paint manufacturers have been trying to phase out oil-based paint for years. But some truths cannot be denied—oil-based paints are extremely durable and, in some applications, unexcelled, especially in kitchens. If your kitchen was last painted with oil-based paint, consider using it again. Oil-based paint can be repeatedly cleaned without the surface wearing away, and it is unaffected by steam and grease.

The downside of oil-based paint is its slow drying time, noxious odor, messy cleanup, and tendency to yellow rapidly (for white hues).

UNDERCOAT, PRIMERS, SEALERS, AND SIZES

Undercoats, primers, sealers, and sizes have specific uses and are important for achieving a good finish. It is seldom appropriate to use paint as a primer. Although numerous types of universal undercoat and primer/sealer are available, always purchase products manufactured by the same company as the top coat and recommended by the manufacturer for the paint you have chosen. Doing so prevents finger-pointing in the rare occasion a problem occurs with the paint.

Several types of primer/sealer are on the market. Bonding primers allowpaint to adhere to glossy or difficult surfaces such as high-gloss paint, varnish, glass, tile, laminate, or paneling, for example. Sealers prevent unwanted stains from bleeding through the finish coats. Undercoats and primers (the terms are used interchangeably) allow adhesion to the underlying surface, provide a suitable surface for finish coats, and prevent porous surfaces from leaching the sheen from glossy top coats. Wallpaper size is used to prepare walls for wall coverings. Size creates an appropriate base for paper, making hanging and future removal easier. A brief list of primer/sealer uses follows:

- New drywall/gypsum board—100 percent acrylic primer or PVA primer

- New plaster/veneer plaster—100 percent acrylic primer

- Old bare plaster—Alkyd primer or 100 percent acrylic primer

- Spackle patches—100 percent acrylic primer

- Old latex paint—100 percent acrylic primer

- Old oil paint—Oil-based undercoat or acrylic primer

- Water stains—Alcohol- or oil-based sealer

- New wood—Oil-based undercoat or 100 percent acrylic primer*

All patches must be primed prior to painting to prevent blemishes in the final coat of paint.

Cedar and redwood contain tannins that bleed through water-based paints. These woods should always be primed with oil- or alcohol-based primer/sealer.

ABOVE Primers and sealers are an important part of achieving a perfect finish. Finish paint does not take the place of the appropriate primer.

ABOVE The variety of surfaces
including plaster, beadboard,
and cabinetry, which have both
latex and oil-based paint surfaces,
makes a bold statement in this
well-designed kitchen.

PREPARATION, PAINTING
AND SPECIAL PROJECTS   29

BULBS & SEEDS

PAINT SHEEN

Paint is available in the following gloss levels (sheens):

- *Matte flat*—No sheen, even from a raking angle

- *Flat*—Generally no sheen, except possibly from a raking angle

- *Eggshell*—Slight sheen seen from a raking angle

- *Satin*—Pronounced sheen but not shiny

- *Semigloss*—Sheen is evident

- *Gloss*—Very shiny, might look wet

Sheen levels vary from manufacturer to manufacturer, as do names for the sheen level. For example, eggshell might be called velvet, or semigloss could be called medium gloss. One company's satin might be as shiny as another's semigloss. Also remember that gloss level increases with additional coats.

In the past, flat paints were avoided in kitchens because they were difficult to clean and intense cleaning left burnish marks on the finish. This is still true of ordinary flat paints, but improved scrubable or washable flat paints are now available for hard-use areas. Still, some degree of sheen level is a plus for hard-use kitchens. Soda spewed on ceilings and grease and food on walls cleans easier from glossy paint than from flat paint.

The condition of your walls and ceilings is another important consideration when choosing paint sheen. Gloss increases the reflectivity of paint, so flat and low-sheen paint tend to hide surface imperfections whereas satin to glossy paints accent imperfections. The degree to which this is true is usually unknown until the finish coats are applied. Thus, a primed surface that looks great might look terrible once finished or might look good during daylight and bad at night under ceiling lighting.

OPPOSITE A satin or semigloss sheen is excellent for hard-use areas. New scrubable flat paints are excellent when a low sheen is desired.

ABOVE The combination of pale yellow paint and distressed blue cabinents creates a bright, engaging room in this sunny cottage.

OPPOSITE Clear finishes protect and highlight natural and stained wood. Shellac, varnish, polyurethane, lacquer, and resin/oil products are all typical clear finish choices.

CLEAR FINISHES

Any discussion of paint must include clear finishes. Although clear finishes are basically paint without the pigment, subtle differences exist in application methods and results. Clear finishes protect and highlight natural or stained wood trim, doors, paneling, floors, and cabinets. Shellac, varnish, polyurethane, lacquer, and resin/oil products are all used for these purposes. There is no perfect finish for every project. Because dozens of products are on the market, choosing the appropriate product for your project can be confusing. A rundown on what's available, what's appropriate, and what's not follows:

Shellac

Shellac, which is formulated by mixing the natural secretions of the Asian lac beetle with alcohol, has been around for centuries. It is a brush-on product that forms a surface film. Shellac is one of the best sealers known and the basis for the renowned French polish method of furniture finishing. Even with the creation of improved varnishes, shellac is still used as the sealer coat for trim, doors, and floors under varnish. Shellac is hygroscopic, meaning that it attracts moisture. Thus, it is a poor choice for damp areas, such as tabletops, kitchens, and bathrooms, where it will blush (turn white). It is also difficult to apply due to its quick drying characteristics. Pigmented shellac is not a clear finish but is an excellent shellac-based sealer.

Varnish

At one time, as many types of varnish were on the paint store shelves as sodas in the grocery store, each formulated for a different purpose. Varnish is a brush-on product that forms a protective surface film. It is a hard-wearing, water-resistant coating that turns amber with age. Basically a mixture of resin, oil, and thinner, varnish is available today but has been largely replaced by tougher, water-resistant polyurethane. Still, varnish has its uses. It is preferred for historic preservation projects and as a finish on softwood floors where harder finishes fail. Do not use varnish as a protective coating over brightly colored decorative finishes—the gradual ambering of the finish drastically affects the underlying color.

Polyurethane

Polyurethane is a cousin to old-fashioned varnish but is harder, more water resistant, and less prone to yellowing. It is a brush-on product that forms a surface film and is available in solvent- and water-borne formulations. Early polyurethane finishes created an unattractive glassy surface coating, and many people still relate that unpopular finish with the modern product. However, modern polyurethane is now indistinguishable from varnish and provides a beautiful finish in a variety of sheens. It is excellent for use in bathrooms and kitchens, on tabletops, hardwood floors, and other areas prone to spills. Exterior polyurethane has ultraviolet absorbers that prevent UV rays from degrading the substrate and should always be used where intense sunlight shines on the finish—including on some interior window sills (stools) to prevent fading and deterioration of the interior surface.

Oil-based polyurethane is more durable than the water-based version, but it is a smelly, slow-drying product. Apply it on hard-use areas, on cabinets near the sink, and on floors around the cooking area or entry doors. Water-based polyurethane emits a light odor and dries quickly. To get a durable finish, apply extra coats. For example, on areas where you would use two or three coats of oil-based polyurethane, use four to six coats of the water-based alternative.

Penetrating Oils and Oil/Resin Finishes

Oil-based finishes penetrate the wood's surface and are excellent for accenting attractive wood grain. You apply these finishes using a brush or a rag. Some are simple oils with dryers added to speed up setting. Others are formulated with resins for improved durability and water resistance. The resulting finish is attractive on furniture, trim, or cabinets where a "country" or early American look is appropriate. Oil-based finishes offer little surface protection from scratches and abrasion, less moisture protection than varnish and polyurethane, and must be renewed over time. Use caution when disposing of the oily rags used with drying oils—they can spontaneously combust and must be taken care of properly. Submerging rags in a bucket of water is a safe method of disposal.

PAINT ADDITIVES

Thinners

Most paint label directions do not recommend thinning or putting additives in the paint; after all, isn't the paint supposed to be perfect from the can? But additives can be useful and make a big difference in the final appearance of a paint job.

In the past, oil-based paints were extremely thick in the can; thinning was required to make the product usable. Modern paints are sold at the consistency recommended for use (after mixing).

- *Wall and Ceiling Paint*—It should not be necessary to thin wall and ceiling paint or primer. Thinning affects coverage and results in runs and sags.

- *Trim Enamels*—The decision to thin trim paint depends on the paint quality, the temperature, and the humidity. When the temperature is hot or the humidity is low or both, enamels dry too quickly. In this case, thinning the paint improves the final appearance and makes application easier. The most basic thinners are water (for latex paints) and mineral spirits (for oil-based paints), but other thinners are available. Note that thinning your paint might make extra coats necessary for optimum coverage and gloss.

- *Proprietary Additives*—The Flood Company manufacturers several paint additives designed to improve the flowing and application qualities of latex and oil-based paint. Floetrol is an additive for latex paints, and Penetrol is an additive for oil-based paint. You can also use mildewcides to inhibit the growth of mildew in damp, troublesome areas.

How Much Paint Do I Need?

Here are some guidelines for determining the amount of paint you will need for a job.

ESTIMATING WALLS AND CEILING PAINT

Most paints cover approximately 350 to 400 square feet (106.7 to 121.9 sq. m) per gallon, depending on the porosity and roughness of the surface. The best way to determine how much paint you need is to measure the wall and ceiling surfaces. Say, for example, that the ceiling of the room to be painted is 18 by 12 feet (5.5 by 3.7 m). Multiplied, this is 216 square feet (20.4 sq. m) to paint. Because a gallon covers about 400 square feet (37.2 sq. m), a gallon definitely is enough to apply one coat but may or may not be enough to apply two coats. If the surface is rough or porous, you will surely need another quart of paint.

Assuming an 8-foot (2.4 m) ceiling, the walls for the room have dimensions of 12 by 8 feet (3.7 by 2.4 m) (times two) and 18 by 8 (5.5 by 2.4 m) (times two) or about 480 square feet (44.2 sq. m), depending on the number of window and door openings. Generally, openings are not reduced from the square footage unless the opening or a brick fireplace consumes the majority of the wall. So, for this room you need about 1¹/₄ gallons for a one-coat job and about 2¹/₂ gallons for a two-coat job. When buying paint, it's better to have too much than too little. This practice saves trips to the store and color-matching problems. Also remember, the cost of 1 gallon of paint compared to the cost of 2 quarts of paint is about the same, so buy the gallon. It's helpful to keep extra paint on hand to touch up stains or damage at a later date. Kitchen areas are especially susceptible to wear and tear due to high traffic and use.

ESTIMATING TRIM PAINT

Estimating the amount of trim paint to purchase is a little more difficult but you use essentially the same process. Figure the square footage of baseboards, doors, trim, windows, and so on before buying paint. A door 3 feet (.9 m) wide and 6 feet, 8 inches (2 m) tall comprises roughly 20 square feet (1.9 square m). Therefore, a quart of paint should be enough to paint two coats on one side of two doors, with plenty to spare. If the baseboard is 8 inches tall (20.3 cm) and the room has approximately 50 linear feet (15.2 m) of baseboard, multiply 50 x 0.66 (8 inches is ²/₃ of 1 foot [30.5 cm]). In this case, you need enough paint to cover about 33 square feet (3.1 sq. m), or 66 square feet (6.1 sq. m) for two coats.

CHAPTER II: GETTING STARTED

Covering Up—How and Why

WHY BOTHER?

Believe it or not, covering up is as important as any part of a paint job. Splatters and drips can ruin floors, cabinets, and furniture; and a previous painter's splatters and drips can mar the results of your hard work. Worse still, a kicked or tipped bucket of paint is catastrophic and can ruin the satisfaction of an otherwise perfect project. Even if you are a good painter, a thorough cover-up is a blessing when the job is over, you're tired, and it's time to clean up. Pull up the tape and paper, wad the plastic, fold the drop cloths, and stand back and admire your work. Here's how the professionals do it.

CLEARING THE SPACE

First, remove all furniture, curtains, lamps, wall hangings, and decorative items that could be damaged or ruined. Move large items to the center of the room, allowing sufficient working space along all walls. When too many large items are in the room to move to the center and provide adequate working space, divide the room in half. Move everything to one side of the room, giving you the freedom to work on the opposite side, then switch the items to the finished side and finish the other half of the room. When you are painting for someone else, the homeowner should move all valuable items to a safe location. Two people should move large furniture to save your backs and prevent damage to furniture legs and the floor.

COVERING UP

A typical cover-up strategy for painting the kitchen follows. First, apply masking tape and paper on the floor at the baseboard—4 inches (10.2 cm) out is adequate, but 6 inches (15.2 cm) is better. Note that tape does not stick to greasy or dusty surfaces. Next, lay drop cloths over the floors, taking care to overlap the perimeter papers. Smooth out all folds and laps in the drop cloths to prevent tripping hazards, and apply a few pieces of tape from the drop cloths to the paper to prevent the cloths from sliding. Drape thin plastic over countertops, furniture, fireplaces, and any remaining items that could get splattered. Cover chandeliers only long enough to paint around them. If you use plastic to do this, make sure the bulbs are cool before you apply the plastic. If the chandelier will be covered for an extended time, tape the light switch in the off position to prevent the plastic from melting onto the bulbs. Mask or cover appliances that could get splattered—refrigerator tops, range hoods, and so on. Protect thermostats and other wall-mounted service boxes with tape. Finally, lay runners on the floors of the rooms approaching your work area to prevent you from walking out paint and dust onto unprotected surfaces.

Covering up also means protecting your clothes and body from paint. Wear old, loose clothing that paint can't hurt and shoes that won't suffer from splatters and smears. Vinyl and nitrile gloves, available at the hardware or paint store, are great for protecting your hands.

ABOVE Thoroughly cover up and mask surfaces before you begin a painting project. You will be glad you did when the job is over. You can quickly pull up the tape and paper, wad the plastic, fold the drop cloths, and stand back and admire your work.

Cleaning

CLEANSERS AND SOLVENTS

Cleaning surfaces prior to painting is too often omitted. Some surfaces don't need cleaning, but when they do, proper cleaning saves time and the possibility of a disastrous outcome. When possible, identify the stains or material to be removed and tailor the cleaner to them. Avoid toxic solvents for cleaning when a safe cleaner suffices. A list of preferred cleansers for specific stains follows:

- Grease and food prevents paint from adhering to surfaces and can bleed through the final coats. Remove grease with trisodium-phosphate (TSP) and warm water, TSP substitute, or a mild cleanser. Remove food with a mild cleanser, TSP, or window cleaner.

- Nicotine bleeds through latex paints and yellows new paint. Remove nicotine with TSP and warm water.

- Mildew will reoccur if not thoroughly removed. Remove mildew with a solution of one part chlorine bleach and five parts water.

- Paint applied over old wallpaper glue will eventually fail. Remove old glue with wallpaper remover, warm water, and an old towel or scrubbing pad.

- Ink will bleed through multiple coats of latex paint. Don't clean it off— seal it with stain sealer.

- Remove pencil marks with window cleaner or paint over them. Paint covers pencil marks.

- Excessive dust can affect the adhesion of your paint or create a rough surface. Sweep off dust with a brush or vacuum it.

- Floor polishes and liquid wax splashed onto baseboards or shoe moldings prevents paint from adhering. Remove these polishes and waxes with wax remover or lightly sand them off the wood.

RIGHT Appropriate cleaning can prevent a disastrous outcome. Knowing the correct type of cleanser to use makes the job much easier.

Repairs

After the work area is clean and covered, repair all deficiencies that could prevent a good paint job. Some methods and materials for repairing walls are described in the following sections.

Dents and Dings

Repair dents, dings, and nail holes in walls with spackling or joint compound. Most areas require at least two coats, and deep dents might take more. When the final coat is dry, sand it smooth and flush to the surrounding surface with 120-grit sandpaper. Picture frame hangers, molly bolts, and other fasteners frequently create bulges that protrude from the wall. Cut the bulges out with a razor knife or dimple them into the wall with a hammer before filling the dent.

Nail or Screw Pops in Drywall

Resecure all nail or screw pops with one or two new nails or screws near the old one, making sure to get a firm grip into a stud, joist, or sheathing. Secure or remove the popped nail or screw and fill the hole with two coats of spackling or drywall compound. Sand it smooth with 120-grit sandpaper.

Cracks

Fill hairline cracks with spackling or joint compound and sand it when dry. Cracks in drywall are rare, but cracks in plaster are common. Large or long cracks often indicate structural problems that should be diagnosed before making repairs. Repair stable hairline cracks with spackling or joint compound. (A stable crack is one that is not getting bigger or changing seasonally.) Repair minor reoccurring cracks with nylon mesh joint tape and three coats of premixed joint compound feathered to the wall or ceiling. When repairing plaster cracks, press on the plaster at each side of the crack to determine if the plaster is securely attached to the lath. If the plaster moves, secure the side or sides with plaster washers and drywall screws (see illustration, right) to decrease movement. Where possible, drive the screws into studs or joists. When this isn't possible, carefully drive the screws into the wood lath. Next tape and float the tape. Plaster that is exceptionally loose or bulged must be removed.

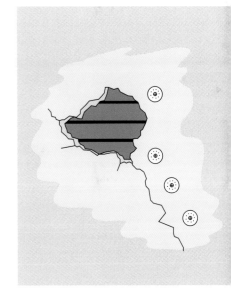

Floating Tape

Floating, sometimes called feathering, is the process of patching by creating a level surface that blends with the adjacent surfaces. To float a surface, liberally apply spackling or drywall compound to a surface, then smooth it out with a trowel or broad knife.

Small Holes

Small holes can be difficult to repair when no backing is present to hold the patching material. Kits are available for these repairs at hardware stores, but you can also use the following methods:

- *Option A:* Cut a scrap piece of drywall or wood that is larger than the hole in two directions but can still be inserted behind the hole. Next, put some construction adhesive on the outer edges of the scrap, and insert it into the hole so that the adhesive bonds the scrap in place. Holding the scrap in place or by temporarily securing it with a taut string, screw drywall screws through the wall to secure the scrap in place until the adhesive dries. Remove the screws and fill the hole with multiple coats of joint compound, or spackling compound until it is flush with the surrounding surface.

- *Option B:* Using a framing square, pencil out a square or rectangle around the hole and cut out the penciled area with a drywall saw. Next, cut a piece of drywall that corresponds to the hole but is about 2 inches (5.1 cm) bigger in all directions. On the back of this larger piece, pencil an outline of the newly cut hole centered on the larger piece. Score the pencil marks with a sharp razor knife and break the scrap at the scores. Peel the perimeter excess away from the front face paper, leaving the center patch piece attached to the facing paper. You should now have a repair piece that will fit into the hole with enough facing paper to secure it to the surrounding intact wallboard or plaster. Before inserting the patch, butter the edges of the hole and the back of the loose paper on the patch with quick-setting joint compound, then insert it into the hole. Smooth the paper around the patch onto the walls with a joint knife and allow the joint compound to dry. When the patch has dried and is secure, float over the whole patch with drywall or spackling compound and sand it flush with the surrounding walls.

BELOW Illustration 1—Use your razor knife or drywall saw to enlarge the existing hole into a perfect square hole, readying it for the patch.

Illustration 2—Insert the patch into the freshly cut hole using a drywall compound.

Illustration 3—A cross–section shows before and after the patch has been inserted into the drywall mud.

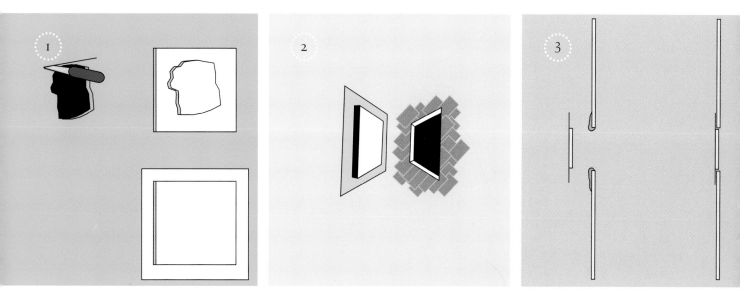

Large Holes

Repair large holes in drywall with a piece of drywall, nylon mesh tape, and joint compound. Using a level and carpenter's framing square, pencil in a square or rectangle around the damaged area, stud-to-stud or joist-to-joist, leaving the framing member on the outside of the line. Remove the damaged drywall along the pencil line with a drywall saw and razor knife. Using a drill, screw pieces of wood (often called nailers) securely onto the existing framing as a base for the repair piece of drywall. Cut a piece of drywall the same thickness as the existing drywall to fit into the hole as perfectly as possible. Insert the piece and secure it with drywall screws. Fill the cracks with joint compound and apply nylon mesh tape over them. Float the tape with at least three coats of premixed drywall compound, taking care to feather the patch onto the wall. Sand it flush with the surrounding surface.

Textured Walls and Ceilings

Old wall and ceiling textures can be difficult to match, but it's possible with appropriately thinned drywall compound and patience. In some cases, it's easier to get rid of the texture by floating over it. To do this, first knock off all high areas and as much of the texture as possible with a stiff blade scraper. (A wallpaper scraper is the perfect tool for this task.) Next, float the area with a 10- to 12-inch (25.4 to 30.5 cm) drywall knife or trowel using a setting-type drywall compound for the first two coats. For the finish coat use premixed joint compound. Sand it smooth with 120-grit sandpaper.

Sand-finish textures are difficult to match, but here are some suggestions. For a fine (sharp) sand finish, add fine silica sand to your joint compound and float over the hole. When the compound dries, lightly rub the path with a damp terry cloth towel to loosen up and reveal the sand.

For sand finishes that have been painted repeatedly, creating rounded humps on the finish, thin enough premixed joint compound with water to create a soupy paintlike mixture. Apply this material over the patch with a roller to approximate the surrounding texture. When dry, lightly knock off the texture peaks with sponge and scrubbing pad. In some cases, a texture roller creates a good match. Many paint stores sell texture roller covers; the surface contains hundreds of small plastic loops. When you can't create the desired texture for a good match, consider retexturing the entire wall, corner to corner.

Plaster

We've purposely avoided giving directions for plastering because it is a process that requires years of experience and skill. It is also difficult to find many of the materials necessary to produce a plaster finish. Most of the wall-repair problems encountered in a kitchen project can be successfully repaired using the techniques and materials already mentioned.

SANDING YOUR REPAIRS

You can sand most wall and ceiling repairs by hand using a small block sander. A pole sander is handy for sanding ceilings with multiple patches. Using a pad sander makes repairs go quickly, but the dust this method creates resembles a forest fire. The fine dust can also ruin your sander. The cleanest method of sanding is to purchase an attachment that connects a sanding pad to your shop vacuum. Your paint store or local rental center might also have these for daily or hourly rental.

TRIM REPAIRS

Repair and prime all trim before applying finish coats of paint. Fill nail holes and dings with spackling and sand it smooth with the adjacent surface. All repairs must be primed to prevent the repair from telegraphing through the painted surface. Use polyester body filler for excessively damaged areas that must be filled or re-formed. When possible, remove thick layers of peeling paint with a heat gun or chemical stripper. Feather-sand small areas of peeling paint. Sand peeling paint adjacent to window glass with a folded piece of 80-grit sandpaper using your finger tips to prevent scratching the glass. Use 220-grit sandpaper for sanding between coats of paint, and use 320-grit sandpaper if the final coat of paint sheen is glossy.

FINAL REPAIRS AND OTHER CONSIDERATIONS

Before the beginning to paint, make all repairs that could affect your paint job.

Doors

Plane or adjust all doors so they close properly. This includes doors that stick due to the settling of the house or heavy paint buildup and doors that drag over carpet.

Windows

Adjust and repair windows so they operate smoothly. Remove excess paint and runs that make windows stick or that affect the weatherproofing of the unit. Retie old or broken sash cords, lubricate metal working parts, and replace broken glass.

Clean Up Sloppy Workmanship

Remove paint slopped on windows, floors, hardware, or appliances by previous painters. Even if the new color is different, this old, sloppy paint will look like it's new and blemish your hard work.

Hardware

Remove or loosen all hardware where you will be painting. Don't attempt to brush around escutcheon plates, knobs, switch plates, and light fixture canopies. This is also a good time to clean, lubricate, and repair these items. When installing new hardware, have it fitted—boring, mortising, and screwing —before painting. Place hardware items with their fasteners in sandwich bags and label them. Note any ruined screws for replacement and wallowed-out screw holes for repair.

OPPOSITE **Adjust and repair all doors before painting them. Also, remove knobs and other hardware to speed up the painting and to get a more attractive finish.**

Wallpaper

It's not a good idea to paint over wallpaper. In the best case, the painted paper will look great, but if the paper ever needs to be removed, you've sealed it in place, making the job difficult or impossible. In the worst case, the paint softens the underlying glue and the paper will begin to bulge and fall as you paint it. Other complications include paint failure over vinyl wall coverings, metallic ornamentation bleeding through the paint, and seams loosening from the wet paint. Some papers, however, can be painted, and special primers are available to use over them for a successful project. Consult with your paint store specialist if you are considering this option.

Application—"Ready To Roll"

Now that it's time to begin painting, arrange all tools and materials—brush, roller frame and cover, pan, extension pole, paint—in a convenient location such as a covered countertop or a table in a room adjacent to the work area. Don't leave the tools underfoot, waiting for a catastrophe.

BOXING THE PAINT

When using more than one gallon of the same paint, it's a good idea to mix the paint together in a larger bucket to ensure that all the paint is exactly the same color. This process is called boxing the paint. Five gallon buckets are good for this purpose. Make sure to clean the paint bucket rims with a damp rag or paper towel after pouring paint. Dry paint on the rim prevents the bucket from closing tightly and allows the paint to harden.

Removing Wallpaper from Bare Drywall

Most interior walls in new construction are covered with gypsum wallboard (also known as drywall, sheetrock, and gyp board). This product is gypsum (a plasterlike material) between two sheets of paper. It's a great product, inexpensive, easy to install, easy to finish, and durable. Unfortunately, many paperhangers—perhaps untrained or on a tight budget—apply new paper or vinyl without first priming and sizing the drywall. The result is basically paper glued over paper, and it's nearly impossible to remove. If the wall covering is vinyl, the paper face of the drywall often pulls off with the vinyl, leaving a difficult mess to repair. If this happens on your project, stop and consult a professional painter or your paint store specialist for advice on how to proceed. In the past, walls ruined in this way could be resurfaced by sealing the damage with oil-based primer and applying a skim coating of quick-setting joint compound. The problem is so common, however, that new products have been introduced to better seal the damage prior to repairs.

CUTTING IN

Painting into the corners and around trim before rolling is called cutting in. Cutting in around corners and ceilings is usually quick work, but cutting in around stained trim, cabinets, or another color is tedious. To begin, pour about one pint of paint into a working bucket. Paint stores sell plastic and metal paint pots for this purpose, but you can also use a clean paint can. Never work from a full gallon of paint. It's too heavy, and if you spill it, all is lost and cleaning up is a nightmare. This process is usually done with a 2½ or 3-inch (6.4 or 7.6 cm) brush. When painting walls and ceilings, paint the ceiling first to prevent splattering ceiling paint down on fresh wall paint. Dip the brush about one-third of the way into the paint, tap it out on the inside of the can, and go. There's no need to pull the paint any farther than it wants to go (called dry brushing). Just be sure to smooth out the paint to prevent runs and heavy brush marks, always looking back every few minutes to make sure your paint is not sagging. About 3 inches (7.6 cm) of cut in area provides ample room to join with the roller.

Painters brush a little ceiling paint down on the wall to provide an overlap area for the wall paint. Straightening lines between colors is usually done with the wall paint. A common problem when brushing and rolling a room is calle hat banding—the unsightly difference between the cut-in and rolled areas of a wall or ceiling. Hat banding is most common when using dark colors or paint that has a sheen. To avoid it, cut in and roll one wall or small area at a time, trying to keep a wet edge between the cut-in area and the rolled area. It also helps to roll as far as possible into the cut-in area without hitting the adjacent surface.

ABOVE Three inches (7.6 cm) of cut-in painting provides plenty of area to join with the roller. It's also a good idea to roll into your wet cut to prevent hat banding.

You can cut in around stained trim or into another color free-handed like a painter or with painter's tape. Free-handed cutting in takes a little more patience and skill but the learning curve is quick. To maintain control of the brush and paint, load the brush with less paint than if you were cutting in walls. Carefully work the bristles to the trim and create a straight line by pulling the brush along in one fluid motion.

Create straight lines with tape by using long lengths and eyeing the tape for true lines. Even when using tape, cut a reasonably neat line into the tape. Too much paint overlapping the tape can damage the paint when the tape is removed. A little paint usually bleeds under the tape; clean this using a damp (not wet) rag pulled tightly over a putty knife.

ROLLING CEILINGS

After cutting in, pour about 1 quart of paint into the roller pan, leaving the upper grid area open. Slowly roll the roller into the paint, across the pan grids, then back into the paint, and so on. This process distributes the paint evenly and saturates the roller cover. Paint should not drip from the cover when you move it from the tray to the wall or ceiling surface.

You can roll ceilings and walls while standing on a ladder, but it's much easier to use a roller extension pole attached into the handle of the roller frame. Poles vary from simple wood broom handles with screw threads to extension poles that allow you to work 12 or more feet (3.7 m) overhead. An extension pole that extends 4 to 6 feet (1.2 to 1.8 m) is adequate for most residential painting.

Seeing the Light

When rolling or brushing, you must have adequate light. A good supply of natural daylight is best, but when daylight is not available, provide plenty of artificial light. Halogen work lights mounted on a stand are best for working in a dark area. Position the lighting to prevent working in shadows. Inspect your work by placing the lights at a raking angle to the painted surface. One warning—two 500-watt halogen lights aimed directly or indirectly at your work might make the walls look insufficiently prepared for painting. But, on second thought, the walls might be prepared perfectly—after all, who's going to inspect them with direct lighting after the job is done? For safety purposes, always turn work lights off when you leave the work area.

When you first contact the ceiling with the roller, lightly roll over about 3 feet (.9 meter) of area to distribute the paint evenly rather than dumping it all in one location. Next, work the paint into areas of about 4 square feet (.4 sq. m), rolling in a W pattern, then fill in all the voids. Before returning to the roller pan for more paint, lightly roll out any heavy areas or lines created by the side of the roller cover. Maintain a wet edge as you move across the ceiling or wall. Keeping a wet edge means that each new roller full of paint joins the wet side of the area just applied to prevent streaking and roller marks. On ceilings, this is best accomplished by rolling across the narrow direction of the room.

WALLS

When the ceiling is finished, prepare to paint the walls. As with the ceiling, pour a small amount of paint into a clean bucket for cutting in at the ceiling and around trim. Using a sash or wall brush, cut in a 2- or 3-inch (5.1 or 7.5 cm) band at the ceiling, in corners, and around trim to join with the roller. Roll the walls just as you did the ceiling, trying to keep a wet edge between your cut in area and the roller. Every few minutes stand back to inspect the walls for runs, sags, roller lines, or holidays—small areas you missed.

ABOVE Distribute the paint evenly over the wall, not all in one place. Occasionally inspect the wall from a raking angle to check for runs or roller lines.

Trim Work

Painting trim takes patience and skill but it is easily learned. If you've never painted trim before, consider asking a friend or contractor to get you started. As with walls, adequate lighting is important. To begin, your work area must be absolutely clean of dust and debris. Any breezes or fans that might stir up dust must be stopped or turned off. Vacuum dust from the trim and floor using a soft brush attachment, taking care to remove dust trapped in cracks, crevices, or woodwork joinery. After vacuuming, it's a good idea to clean the trim with a tack cloth—a lint-free piece of sticky cheesecloth designed to remove all traces of dust from painted surfaces. As the cloth fills with dust, fold the used side in and continue with a fresh part of the cloth. Tack cloths are inexpensive and available at most paint stores.

A 2½ inch (6.4 cm) angular sash brush is usually adequate for painting trim. Use a wider brush for wide trim, such as that found in a historic home, or slab doors, and a narrower brush for casement windows with dainty details.

PRIMING

Apply your primer as smoothly as possible—no brush marks, runs, and sags —even though you will sand it before the first coat of paint. When possible, fill all holes and dents and sand them smooth before priming. Do not caulk before priming; dry primer makes a great base for the caulk and helps the caulk adhere to the surface better than if it is applied to raw materials. If you are using old paint or primer, strain the material through a paint strainer or the leg of an old pair of nylon pantyhose.

ABOVE Apply primer as smoothly as possible, brushing in the direction of the wood grain. Avoid lapping paint in the wrong direction over joinery intersections unless using you are using a slow-drying material.

To Paint or Not To Paint

Painting switch and receptacle plates is controversial. Yes, they look better painted the same color as the wall, and, yes, they also soil more quickly than the wall. It's your decision. To paint plastic, nylon, or metal plates, first sand them thoroughly to remove any gloss and provide a good base for paint adhesion. Next, apply at least two coats of enamel. To paint the screws, punch holes in a piece of cardboard, push the screws in the holes, then paint them while holding the cardboard.

Begin by pouring a small amount of primer into a clean paint pot or bucket. Using a small working bucket prevents spilling a full bucket and allows you throw away small amounts of leftover or contaminated primer. If you haven't used this primer before or are unfamiliar with painting techniques, begin on test panels of old trim or cardboard to get a feel for the primer and brush. Primer seldom needs to be thinned, but in unusually hot or dry weather adding a little water to water-based primers or mineral spirits to oil-based primers improves the brushability and reduces brush marks by allowing the paint to flow smoothly. Always thin paint sparingly—for example, begin by adding about 1 tablespoon of the appropriate thinner to one pint of paint.

Apply your primer in the direction of the wood grain. If the wood grain is not evident, it usually runs the long distance of a piece of trim, for example, vertically down the stiles of a door and horizontally across the rails. When the area is covered—and before moving to the next area—straighten and smooth your brushstrokes in one long sweep. Respect trim joinery with your brushstrokes by stopping squarely at all joinery intersections.

When using slow-drying oil-based primers and paints, you can blend any excess paint into subsequent brushing; with fast-drying water-based paints, you must control overlaps to prevent them from telegraphing through subsequent layers of paint. Most painters control overlaps with a damp rag wrapped around their finger or a putty knife. You can also use painter's tape at joinery intersections. Some suggestions for painting various trim and door features in the average room follow.

Paneled Doors

When painting paneled doors, begin with panels, starting at the upper panels and moving down. When painting panels, always load your brush with paint sparingly and start at the upper side of the panel to prevent runs at the bottom of the panels. In most cases, the paint should be brushed vertically. When the panels are finished, paint the center rail and vertical mullion that usually forms the cross in the middle of the door. Do not allow excess paint to roll over onto the painted panels, and remember to pull out your brush marks with long even strokes before moving to the next area.

Next, paint the horizontal upper and bottom rails, then paint the vertical stiles. If you are confused about painting the door edges—the lock edge and the hinge edge—there is a steadfast rule for proceeding. Standing in the room you are painting, open the door. If the door opens into the room you are painting, paint the lock edge the color of the door. If the door opens away from the room you are painting, paint the hinge edge. You can create a

Anatomy of a Panel Door

Panel 1, 2, 3, 4
Muntin. 5, 6
Head Rail 7
Lock Rail. 8
Bottom Rail 9
Lock Stile 10
Hinge Stile. 11

straight painted edge by taking a damp rag (moistened with paint thinner or water, whichever is appropriate) and carefully sliding it with your finger down the painted and unpainted junction. Painting the door stop corresponds to the door—adjacent room colors should not be evident in the freshly painted room when the door is closed, and the new paint should not be evident in the adjacent room when the door is closed. When finished, always inspect your work a few minutes later to check for runs or sags.

If your doors are new, they should be primed or sealed with at least one coat of paint on the top and bottom sides. You might think this going a little too far, but if the doors warp (yes, it happens), the manufacturer will blame the problem on the painter and void the warranty.

Slab Doors

A slab door has one flat face with no panels or relief. Slab doors are easy to paint using a 3-inch (7.5 cm) wall or trim brush and working vertically from top to bottom, moving across the door to keep a wet edge as you go. Sometimes, however, the room conditions do not allow you to keep a wet edge and brushing results in heavy brush marks and unsightly overlaps. Avoid these problems by using a 6-inch (15.2 cm), low-nap miniroller. These inexpensive rollers are available at most paint stores and make quick work of large, flat areas. Many of these rollers apply the paint so smoothly that subsequent brushing is unnecessary.

Blocking—What Is It and Why You Should Care

One of the attributes of modern water-based paint is its flexibility. This characteristic allows the paint to stretch and bend with the substrate, despite changes in the temperature and humidity. Oil-based paints are just the opposite; they become brittle with age, an inherent quality that eventually prevents the paint from moving with the substrate, resulting in paint failure. However, there is no perfect one size fits all product. The materials that make water-based paints flexible (a good thing) also create a problem known as blocking (a bad thing). Blocking occurs when two surfaces painted with water-based paints touch and stick together, over and over and over. Blocking occurs on cabinet doors, windows, and screens. There's a good chance that your paint salesman will never have heard of this problem, but manufacturers are well aware of it and are working to alleviate it. The best solution is to use top-quality enamels only. It also helps to make sure all sticking doors, drawers, windows, and so on are in good working order before painting.

WINDOWS

There are too many types of window to discuss separately here, but a few window-painting basics can prepare anyone for this often-dreaded task. Some basic rules and facts follow:

• Do not paint weather stripping, sash cords, pulleys, hardware, or any metal or vinyl parts. Painting these items affects the workability of the window unit.

• Do not close the windows when the paint is still wet. Doing so makes the windows stick shut and mars the painted surfaces.

- Windows that are marginally operative from excessive layers of paint only become worse with added coats of paint.

- Paint windows in a careful sequence—do not stray from this sequence.

- Never apply full brushloads of paint at the junction of the moveable sash and the fixed stops. Doing so can make the window stick.

- Do not worry about getting paint on glass.

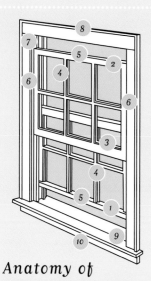

Anatomy of a Double-hung Window

Painting Double-Hung Windows

If your house is more than 30 years old, there's a good chance it has double-hung windows. Double-hung means that the upper sash pulls down and the lower sash pushes up. There's also a good chance that your upper sash is painted shut. If it isn't painted shut, use the following procedure to paint it. First, move both sashes up and down to free up the movement. Then, pull the upper sash down and push the lower sash up so that the bottom rail of the lower sash is a few inches above the meeting rail of the upper sash. In this position, begin on the upper sash: paint the lower muntins, meeting rail, and at least 2 inches (5.1 cm) of the side muntins and stiles. When you have completed this, push up the upper sash, leaving it open about 1 inch (2.5 cm) from the top. Paint the muntins of the upper sash first, beginning with the upper sides, progressing to the flanking sides, and finishing with the bottom side. This order is important—if you paint a lot of windows, you'll surely discover areas that were not prepped adequately, and you do not want paint flakes or sanding dust to fall down onto wet paint. Next, pull the lower sash down, leaving it open from the bottom by about 1 inch (2.5 cm), and paint it. Do not close the windows until they are dry, and always move them up and down a few times the next day to ensure they work smoothly.

When the sashes are painted, paint the sash stops, head casings—including the unseen top edge—side casings, stool, and apron.

If your upper sash does not work and you do not want to free it up, you can still paint the inaccessible meeting rail—here's the secret. The visible part of the upper meeting rail is impossible to access easily if the upper sash does not move. Paint this seemingly inaccessible strip using a thin painter's pad. The Warner Tool Company makes a handy pad they call a Bender Pad because it can be bent to adapt to any oddball location. Other pads also work, but you can make your own with a painter's pad and piece of metal.

Three Ways to Paint around Glass

Painters who paint windows quickly, neatly, and efficiently are highly valued in the trade. These sought-after painters always use an angled sash brush, making two swift strokes down each muntin without a trace of paint on the glass, with the exception of a scant $1/32$ inch (0.8 mm) to create a paint seal between the sash and the glass. (This paint seal is very important on the exterior, less so on the interior.) With the right tool and patience, you can learn to do this at an acceptable speed in a short time. It's a gratifying skill that allows you to stand in one place, have a soda, listen to the radio, and carry on a conversation at the same time. If this doesn't appeal to you—say, you never intend to paint another window the rest of your life—you can tape the glass. And there's one more way, although it pains me to reveal it: Simply slop paint onto the glass, let it dry, and scrape it off later with a single-edged razor blade.

Casement Windows

Casement windows usually open out either with a crank or a sliding adjuster. Steel casement windows were popular during the first half of the twentieth century; wooden casements have been used throughout the twentieth century and are popular today. Some casements are equipped with interior screens or winter storm window fittings that must be painted with the window.

As with other windows, the casement sash must be opened for painting. Old casements are generally easy to paint, beginning at the top and moving down, taking care to keep paint off moving parts, weather stripping, and the exterior sides and edges of the sash and frame. Painting new casements is a little harder because the working mechanisms are complicated—don't paint working parts and don't leave bare wood that can swell from ambient humidity. Paint areas that are difficult to reach with a thin artist's brush. If these areas are apparent, prime and paint them until they look acceptable. If they don't show, prime them and forget about it. You can disconnect some casement sashes easily from their cranking hardware, which makes them easier to paint. When painting wooden casement sashes, old or new, be sure to paint the top edge that opens out because this area is vulnerable to rain penetration.

LEFT Paint windows with an angled sash brush. A narrow paint seal between the sash and glass protects the wood and paint from premature deterioration.

LEFT Create straight lines between colors either by hand or by using masking tape. Straighten crooked lines after the paint dries.

CUTTING A STRAIGHT LINE

Cutting a straight line between two colors is among the hardest of trimming tasks. Bumpy old paint, caulk, and uneven walls or ceilings make a difficult task even harder. Professional painters do this with a steady hand, a good brush, and a keen eye. To begin, the wall paint should slightly overlap onto the trim. Then, using an angled sash brush, pull the paint down the edge in the longest strokes possible. The paint should cover the wall paint overlap, but should not extend out onto the wall surface. If the paint drifts over onto the wall, clean it off with a rag dampened with the appropriate thinner and pulled tightly over a putty knife. When the trim paint dries, further straighten lines with the wall paint as necessary. By now you've proba- bly guessed that creating straight lines can also be accomplished using masking tape. Beware, however, because tape can pull off your new wall paint, so if you choose to use tape, use painter's tape for sensitive surfaces only.

STAINING

Staining new trim, doors, or cabinets can be tricky, so we've included some helpful hints to make the process easier, beginning with a few basics.

• Always stain and finish bare wood prior to painting to prevent paint from being absorbed into the wood. Clean all pencil marks, fingerprints, and dirt from cabinets before staining; stain does not disguise these blemishes. Sand all sharp corners (arrises) to allow better penetration of the stain and to prevent stain from being worn away during subsequent sandings. The process of sanding the arrises is also known as easing or crowning the edges.

• Always prepare a stain sample on the same kind of wood that you will be sanding to see if the stain appears as you intend. Some soft woods, such as pine, absorb a lot of stain and may appear too dark. Some hardwoods, such as maple, absorb very little stain and may appear too light. Many woods do not absorb stain evenly, resulting in a blotchy appearance. Remedy this problem by using a prestain conditioner before staining. Prestain conditioners partially seal the wood and usually prevent a blotchy, uneven appearance.

• Stains are available in water-based and oil-based formulations. Always read the directions to be sure that the stain and subsequent clear protective coats are compatible.

• Apply stain in small areas, then wipe it off with clean, absorbent rags before moving to other areas. For example, stain the side of a door side, wipe off the excess, then stain the other side. Or, stain cabinet doors and wipe off the excess stain, one at a time. Stain and wipe cabinet frames separate from the doors. Never partially stain an area and quit before finishing the whole area.

• Apply stain with a brush, making sure to cover all surfaces including nooks and crannies.

• Always take a close second look at your staining before applying a clear coat. After the clear coat is applied, it is difficult to touch up missed areas.

• Always submerge rags used with oil-based stains in a bucket of water to prevent spontaneous combustion.

• Allow oil-based stains to dry for at least one day before you apply a clear finish. Water-based stains dry quickly and can be clear-coated the same day.

APPLYING CLEAR FINISHES ON NEW WORK

As with final coats of paint, preparation and cleanliness is crucial in getting a smooth finish when using clear finishes. A clean work area, without breezes and passersby, and tacking of the surface is crucial. On new work and according to the manufacturer's instructions, the first coat is usually either a thinned version of the finish product or a sanding sealer. When appropriate, sanding sealer seals the porosity of the wood and provides an excellent film for sanding to a glasslike surface. Never mix a clear finish (except for oils) by shaking the can. This method creates air bubbles in the finish that can mar your finish.

Clear finishes are a little more difficult to apply than paints because they are generally thinner and are prone to creating runs. Also, because they are clear, it is sometimes difficult to see the difference between the coated and uncoated surfaces. Adequate lighting is the key to a good finish. For a final inspection, use a raking light (a light held at an angle to the surface) to reveal holidays, runs, or sags that must be corrected before moving on. As the finish dries, the wet appearance dulls and random areas look like holidays (skips) in the finish. Do not attempt to brush out these areas or any setting sags or runs; make repairs after the finish is dry.

Apply the first coat or sealer with a clean, high-quality brush that has not been used in paint—pure bristle for oil-based products and synthetic bristle for water-based products. Dip your brush partially into the finish, patting out the excess on the side of the can. As with paint, flow the finish on in the direction of the wood grain and smooth out any overlaps or diagonal brush marks with a long, sweeping motion before moving to another area. When dry, sand the sealer with 220-grit sandpaper, and tack the surface clean before applying the first finish coat. If you have nail head holes to fill, apply colored putty in the holes over the dry sealer.

Two finish coats applied over the sealer and sanding between coats with 320-grit sandpaper is standard procedure. Apply the finish sparingly, taking care to cover all areas. Remember to inspect your work with a raking light when it is dry.

APPLYING CLEAR FINISHES OVER OLD WORK

When old finishes are scratched and dull you can sometimes rejuvenate them with a new coat of finish. The first step is to determine if any waxes or oils containing silicone have been used, because they can affect the adhesion and appearance of the new coat of finish. To do this, apply some of the new finish to a small, discrete area, let it dry, and then attempt to scratch the new coating off with your fingernail or pull it off with masking tape. If the finish does not tenaciously cling to the old finish, if it will not dry, or if the new surface dries with a blotchy appearance, the old finish must be thoroughly cleaned. If the test patch did not dry but otherwise looks good, the surface is probably covered with wax. Remove wax with a wax remover, then wipe the surface with a cloth dampened in VMP naptha (a fast-drying paint thinner), changing rags or towels frequently to remove rather than smear the contaminant. Always scuff the surface with 220-grit sandpaper to provide "tooth" for the subsequent coating.

The worst contaminant of all is silicone, which is often an ingredient in various polishes, oils, and rejuvenators. Silicone causes fisheyes, ugly blemishes that look like little craters on the finish. Silicones are difficult to remove, and solvents are ineffective against them. Careful cleaning with ammonia may work; you can also apply a thin coat of shellac to seal the surface. Professional finishers usually add a little fisheye eliminator to their finish to solve the problem. This eliminator is available at auto-finishing stores and works by adding silicone to the new finish, thus relieving the surface tension between the contaminated surface and the new coating.

ABOVE Good lighting is a must when applying clear finishes. Daylight is best, but strategically placed halogen lights are a close second. In this photograph, the author is using a portable light to check for holidays in the varnish

OPPOSITE Painting is an affordable way to spruce up a kitchen without having to invest in new cabinets. You can restrict the painting to just the doors and cabinetry frame, or paint the interiors the same color or a different color for added pizzazz.

Chapter III: Special Considerations

So far, we've discussed the basics of interior painting without getting into anything unusual or particularly challenging. This chapter covers a few more difficult or unusual projects in your kitchen project. We begin with areas you may not have thought about painting and finish with suggestions for decorative paint finishes.

Painting Cabinets

If your kitchen has dark wooden cabinets, metal cabinets, or stained or painted cabinets that are worn and ugly, painting them could be an affordable and attractive method to spruce up the room without dropping a fortune on new cabinets. Your first decision is to determine if the cabinets are worth the investment of your time. Hand-built, solid wood or plywood cabinets are usually great candidates for repainting. On the other hand, if your cabinets are pressed wood or laminate, painting might be a waste of time. In this case, if the frames are sturdy, consider purchasing new doors.

You can paint the entire cabinet, including the interiors, or simply paint the doors and face frames—this is your decision. You must also decide whether to replace hinges, pulls, and knobs. If your new choice of hardware does not match up to the old hardware holes, these holes must be filled and the new holes drilled and doors refitted before painting.

It's best to remove doors and drawers for painting. Doing so frees up the space for painting the frames and interiors. Also, by painting the doors laid flat, you'll do a better job. One way to do this effectively is to stretch two long pieces of 2- by 4-foot (61 by 121.9 cm) framing lumber between ladders or tables to create a platform for painting the doors.

Preparation begins with cleaning all food, oil, and grease off the various elements. TSP works great for this chore. Cabinet doors near the kitchen range are sometimes exceptionally greasy; a little acetone on a rag can remove the last traces of grease from the wood's pores. After cleaning the cabinets, every area must be sanded thoroughly to ensure that the new paint adheres to the old finish. Sand the old finish by hand with 120-grit sandpaper or use a pad or random-orbit sander, changing the paper frequently. When finished, vacuum the dust and finish with a tack cloth.

Most cabinets require a coat of primer and two coats of enamel. Satin and semigloss enamels are the most popular sheens because they stand up to frequent cleaning. If you are painting the cabinet interiors, do it first. A 6-inch (15.2 cm) mini roller speeds up the painting. A brush with a short or cut-off handle is often necessary to reach every nook and cranny. Next, paint the face frames, just as recommended for wood trim. Brush, roll, or spray cabinet doors. Whichever method you choose, it works best to position the doors horizontally. This prevents runs and sags and allows the paint to flow out as much as possible. If brushing, be sure to pull your brush marks straight and smoothly from end to end. If rolling, avoid a roller cover that leaves an exceptionally stippled surface.

Allow the cabinets and frames to dry thoroughly before installing hardware and reattaching the doors. When reattaching, place a moving pad or blanket below the door to prevent scratching the surface.

Painting Floors

Painting kitchen floors is not a new practice, but it fell out of favor with the introduction of inexpensive linoleum and vinyl sheet flooring. Older kitchens frequently have softwood floors, and all types of wood floors are now commonly installed in new kitchens. Like any architectural surface, wood floors can be painted. Besides using a single paint color, other options include stenciling, marbleizing, wood graining, lining (striping), tromp l'oeil, and any combination of these finishes.

When painting a wood floor, you'll get the best results on bare wood and less satisfactory results on old polyurethane or varnish. Have old floors sanded by a professional floor sander, or do it yourself using rental equipment or a high-quality belt sander and random-orbit sander. Either way, protect other areas of the house with plastic and tape to contain the dust. Also, make sure there is no asbestos in remaining linoleum adhesives or lead in remaining paint. If so, special procedures should be taken to abate these toxic materials.

LEFT Colorful stripes on the floor tie in other design elements in the room.

Vacuum all the dust, taking care to suck dust from the cracks between boards that could be pulled up by your brush. Next, tack the floor clean. When using water-based paint, prime the floor with a thin coat of 100 percent acrylic primer. When using oil-based paint, prime the floor with a thinned coat (15 to 20 percent) of the finish paint. Floor and deck enamel is the best choice for painting floors. Because it is unlikely that you'll choose a standard premixed color for your kitchen floor, locate a paint company that can mix the floor paint that you want. You'll have a choice of oil-based or water-based paint. Water-based floor and deck enamels usually dry with a flat or low sheen; oil-based floor and deck enamels usually dry with a high gloss finish. Low sheen water-based paint tends to hold dirt and is hard to clean unless it is clear coated. Glossy oil-based paint is slick—which is inappropriate as a base for subsequent stenciling and other decorative painting techniques. An alternative to glossy oil-based floor and deck enamel is satin industrial enamel. If none of these products fits into your plan, paint the floor with interior satin oil-based enamel and allow several days for drying before using the floor.

Painting Countertops

Laminate countertops and backsplashes can also be painted. The finish will not be as hard and as durable as the original finish, but you can preserve it by using cutting boards and trivets to protect the final surface. To paint a laminate countertop, first secure any loose edges or pieces with laminate adhesive. Prepare the surface by cleaning it thoroughly and wet sanding with 220-grit wet-or-dry sandpaper until all traces of a surface gloss are removed. Wipe the surface clean, and provide a final cleaning with a tack cloth.

A lot of primers on the market claim to adhere to any surface. The primer you select must be a bonding primer and appropriate for use under the final finish. Two good choices for a durable finish are satin sheen industrial enamel or epoxy—both dry very hard. The application technique you use is also important because you don't want the finish to look like it was brushed. Use a quality 6-inch (15.2 cm) miniroller to apply the paint evenly, beginning on a sample board to make sure the material is thinned appropriately and flows out adequately. Once the final coat is dry, it can be further decorated to resemble granite, marble, or any other effect.

ABOVE Color-washing highlights the wall texture and adds its own textural effect to this room. Decorative wall finishes also provide their own textural qualities and can be used to unite dissimilar colors between rooms.

OPPOSITE Painted stripes are a great way to create the look of wallpaper, using any color combination imaginable.

Painting Tile

The methods for painting glazed tile are similar to those for painting glass. The slick surface must be roughened up with sandpaper to create an appropriate surface for painting. As recommended for laminate, wet-or-dry sandpaper is best, followed by a bonding primer and a hard, durable paint. You can re-create grout lines using an artist's brush and a solvent-dampened rag to clean up crooked lines.

Painting Appliances

Appliances such as refrigerators can be painted to look as good as new by spraying them with automotive enamel. This project, however, is not for do-it-yourselfers and should be done by a spray professional. Do not paint your electric or gas range; the heat generated by these appliances can discolor the paint.

Decorative Finishes

Many books have been published about decorative possibilities, applications, and varieties of decorative painted finishes. Most of us now refer to these techniques as faux finishes, faux being the French word for false or not real. For example, faux marble (or faux marbre) is a painted imitation intended to look like real marble. For our purposes, we mention a few options for your kitchen that add interest, intrigue, coordination, and texture to an otherwise boring or ordinary paint scheme. Create faux finishes to decorate walls that can compete with or surpass expensive wallpapers in appearance. You can also use faux finishes to disguise rough, blemished walls and trim.

Not that long ago, few people knew what faux finishes were, and precious little information about the techniques was available, with even fewer artisans who could apply them. This has all changed, and today excellent do-it-yourself kits, materials, and tools are on the market, which allow anyone with a little imagination and experience to create a great look for a little money.

THE BASICS

The basis of most faux finishes is an opaque painted base and one or more transparent coats (sometimes called glazes) applied over the base coat and manipulated to create the desired effect. The tools to create the final effects vary from technique to technique. A few finishes you can use on walls, trim, cabinets, or anywhere you want follow. You are limited only by your imagination.

BASE COATS

The base coat for most finishes is simply a coat (or coats) of paint that shows through the subsequent glazes. On walls, all blemishes are repaired and primed, and the base coat of paint is rolled on, just as for any wall paint.

Base coats on trim and doors must be exceptionally smooth to prevent brush or roller marks from telegraphing through the final finishes.

When using water-based glazes, use water-based base coats. When using oil-based glazes, use oil-based base coats. Whichever you choose, it's a good idea to scuff up the surface with fine sandpaper before applying the glaze.

Choosing a Base Color

Because base coats show through the glazes, your choice of color is important and must be compatible or harmonize with subsequent glazes.

Some simple combinations are listed below.

BASE COAT	GLAZE COAT
Off-white	Umber, ocher, blues, greens, reds, yellows
Blue	Umber, contrasting blues, blue-green
Pink	Pale umber, reds, contrasting pink, whites
Brown	Off-whites, contrasting browns, ocher, yellow
Red	Off-whites, contrasting reds or pinks, umber, black
Yellow	Off-whites, contrasting yellows, ocher,
Terra-cotta	Off-whites, umber, ocher, green, red

The previous combinations are classic combinations. Other palettes and layering of colors can also have exciting and unexpected results, such as the following possibilities:

BASE COAT	GLAZE COAT
Yellow	Reds and pinks creating variations of orange
Blue	Yellow to create greens
Pink or red	Blues to create purple or lilac

Obviously, this list can go on and on, according one's taste and decorating scheme.

The sheen of the base coat is important because it affects the final finish. Most decorative painters use a low sheen (eggshell or satin) enamel for base coats. If the paint is too glossy, the glazes might not adhere well. If the paint is too flat, the base might absorb too much of the color and prevent easy manipulation of the glaze.

GLAZE AND TOP COATS

The medium used over the base coat can be a transparent glaze or thin paint. Glazes are formulated to keep a wet edge longer than thinned paints. They are available in water-based and oil-based formulation. They can be made from scratch using various materials such as varnish, boiled linseed oil, and paint. If you are a novice painter, keep it simple and stick to the store-bought formulas rather than trying to make your own.

Many paint stores now sell tinted glazes that make the whole selection and buying process easy. Your paint clerk can also alter these selections with universal colors. If you prefer to start from scratch, buy untinted glazing liquid and have it mixed to the color you desire. The pigment-to-glaze ratio determines how opaque or transparent the final glaze is.

You can create many finishes by simply thinning the desired color of paint and applying it over the base coat. In some cases, this method works fine. However, there's a fine line between a paint thinned to create a semitransparent effect and a paint thinned so much that it runs off the brush like water. In this case, the addition of a little glazing liquid thickens the mixture (adds body) enough for manipulation.

Some Final Thoughts

Whether painting a piece of furniture or your whole house, always save the leftover paint for touch-ups. If a substantial part of the gallon or quart remains unused, clean the top and place the lid on tightly. If a small amount of paint is left, put it in a smaller container (such as mustard jar) in which it will not dry up. Always label your paint with the name and date applied, and smear a dab across the top for reference. Store remaining paint where it will not freeze.

It's also a good idea to keep a card file or notebook of all the colors used during a project. Notes should include the name of the color and color chip, the color formula (ask for an extra adhesive label), the brand name of the paint, the store where it was purchased, and, finally, the date. You'll be pleased to have this if the leftover paint disappears or if you must rummage through 50 cans of paint looking for right one to match.

COLOR PALETTES

Introduction

Painting your kitchen is probably the easiest, most economical way to achieve a dramatic new look—without pricey and time-consuming renovations. By following the instructions in Section 1 of this book, you can transform any or all of this room's important elements. But one question remains: which color is perfect for your kitchen?

Because the kitchen plays a round-the-clock role in most households—for the cook, for the kids doing homework around the table, for entertaining guests—its color is as crucial a design element as its appliances and storage space. This room must work well and look great. So, in this section, you'll see a wide range of palettes that perform color magic in all kinds of settings— from traditional to trendy.

Your Inspiration

Choosing great kitchen colors is often a matter of looking around—at the other rooms of your home, prized possessions, the outside landscape (if there's a view), even your wardrobe. From this informal survey, you will probably notice that the same colors appear again and again. Consider these favored hues for your painting plan.

If you do not intend to change certain elements of your kitchen, look at them as part of the final palette. For example, if you've chosen stainless steel appliances, consider silvery gray as one of your colors. Do likewise with finished wood. Depending on the stain, wood can have a yellow, orange, red, brown, or even black tone. Factor these hues into your chosen palette to ensure the most pleasing effects.

Finish Facts

Because airborne grease, food particles, and smoke adhere to painted finishes, use paint in semigloss or high-gloss for easy cleaning. If you like a matte finish, use flat finish paint or milk paint, then protect the surface with a compatible clear, matte sealer—usually polyurethane—which is easy to clean. Your paint dealer can help you choose the specific sealer for your paint type.

OPPOSITE An ocean view moves inside, with a kitchen that reflects the colors of sky and surf.

The Blue Room

Why do so many people choose blue as their favorite color? Perhaps this affinity stems from human's primal need for water. Psychologists who have studied color notice the calming effect it produces. In any case, blue shows up in the kitchen more often than any other hue.

Blue combines beautifully with many other colors and materials. Brushed steel, brass, and copper shimmer in its company. Wood, which glows naturally in shades from yellow to red, is seen by the eye as the opposite of blue; this complementary relationship is also pleasing and harmonious. And the popularity of blue and white pottery and tile—in many cultures—attests to a multinational love affair with this color combination.

In a traditional kitchen, carefully detailed custom cabinetry is enhanced by a finish of blue milk paint, hand-applied by professionals; the delicate paint is then protected by a catalyzed top coat and sealer. Because this blueberry shade is a deeply saturated color, the designers have used expanses of white in the work areas and good task lighting to promote visibility. Natural wood details with an orange cast—wide-plank flooring, a rough-hewn support post and beam, a scrubbed-top table—create a handsome counterpoint to the broad expanse of color created by the blue cabinetry.

Using a warm blue, like the country hue chosen for the open plan kitchen, right, softens the stark, vertical lines of this high-ceilinged space. Wood floors and patterned ceramic tile on the backsplash complete the traditional look without sacrificing the room's light, airy feeling.

Wall space above the cabinets provides a wonderful opportunity for display, and it is also a great spot for storing items that are used infrequently. Decorative platters, large bowls, and other awkwardly sized tableware find a secure home in this location.

To add height to low ceilings, always paint wall or soffit space above the cabinets to match the ceiling color.

RIGHT Periwinkle blue panel doors are in contrast with the white walls and ceiling of this inviting kitchen. The warmth of the wood flooring and marigold cabinet interior offsets the cooler colors.

CREATING CONTRASTS

Because it dwells on the cool side of the spectrum, blue softens the effect of bright strokes of color. Whereas pink paint on the walls and ceiling provide a bold backdrop in this traditionally styled kitchen, opposite, blue cabinets—paired with stainless steel appliances and hardware and gray laminate counters—provide balance with the warmer hue. Blue and coral tiles, set in a pleasing pattern above the range, display the palette and prove how well opposites work together. Notice how the use of this combination makes stock cabinets and a basic layout look fresh and contemporary.

When blue is the predominate color in a kitchen, things can get chilly, particularly if the room has a lot of smooth, reflective surfaces. Modernist designers were aware of the effect of hard surfaces and crisp edges, often balancing severe geometry and monochromatic color schemes with a dash of contrasting color and texture—usually in the form of upholstery, carpet, or other textiles.

To achieve a glamorous look in a minimalist space, the designers took an economical product—mass-produced stock cabinets from IKEA—and customized them with a coat of gleaming blue paint, courtesy of their local auto body shop. The high shine and hard metallic edges of this kitchen, opposite, enhance its sleek feel, but the designers impart warmth to the scheme with seating upholstered in a lively orange fabric.

HOT TIPS FOR COOL SPACES

Cool colors—blues and grays—and appliances and trims in silver tones are always refreshing in warm climates, or in summer when the mercury soars. But too much chill on an icy winter day may make you want to reach for a sweater. To warm up a space, add decorative accents in warm hues: reds, oranges, sunny yellows. Use textiles, tableware, or floral arrangements in warm colors to turn up the heat in a cool room.

Primarily Colorful

We often associate the pure, bright hues of red, yellow, and blue with children. Many toy companies use this palette, as do juvenile furniture manufacturers and picture book publishers. But these colors are not just for kids; seeing this happy combination in a kitchen can also lift grownup spirits.

Imagine a tired, tiny kitchen with old-fashioned fixtures, done up in a peeling coat of "landlord white" paint. Sometimes, tenants need more fun! With the owners' permission, the renters of a small, city flat transformed their cooking space, opposite, with a few pints of primary red, yellow, and blue, defining some of the room's trim and angles with a couple coats of black.

Although conventional wisdom would caution against the use of brilliant color in a small space, the counterintuitive genius of this kitchen is that its colorfulness has transformed what was a dull, unappealing, and cramped room into a fun place to congregate. While the dimensions are cozy, there's no doubt that guests will remember this kitchen with a smile.

TIPS FOR USING MULTIPLE BRIGHT COLORS

If you are considering using two or three bright colors in a confined space, work out the paint layout in advance:

• Take a picture of the space and make several blown-up black and white photocopies. Using corresponding colored pencils or markers, color in the areas to be painted to find an arrangement of color that pleases your eye.

• When you're using a stencil or a complicated, multicolor pattern for a floor or wall, sketch or copy it on paper and color it with markers or pencils in your chosen hues. It's a great way to avoid mistakes when you're down on the floor or up on the ladder, brushes in hand.

Using the dominant colors of their collection of culinary accessories, the homeowners decided to pull together a group of flea-market finds to create a cohesive color palette for their kitchen and dining area. Yellow walls brighten these combined spaces, and old furnishings get a new incarnation with the application of high-intensity primaries.

Capitalizing on its square dimensions and rectilinear shelves, the paint job begins with a primary-hued, geometric quilt pattern for the floor, rendered in a hard-working, high-gloss sheen.

White walls and shelves in the pantry tame the intensity of all the primary details, acting as a framework for the colorful setting.

OTHER WAYS TO USE PRIMARY COLORS

Using pure, vibrant red, yellow, and blue creates a classic combination for the kitchen, but you have other ways to create a palette with this triad. Go shopping in the paint chip section of your paint store to try related primary schemes.

Consider pastel tints of the primaries—light, buttery yellow walls with baby-boy blue cabinets, and accents of pink for kitchen linens, glassware, and furniture. Or go in the opposite direction, choosing deeply saturated shades: burgundy, navy, and rich gold.

PAINT AS A BOUNDARY

Architects working with large-volume spaces—loft residences, artists' studios, and the like—often carve up a big floor plan in decidedly untraditional fashion. Because daylight enters such a space through exterior walls only, the designer must be creative to avoid the problem of a dark, cavernous core. Reflective surfaces—metal and large expanses of white—as well as transparent features such as glass blocks and one-half- or three-quarter-height walls help transmit light from the perimeter to the center. In such constructions, boundaries and borders can be set by the effective use of color; using bright hues often counteracts a low-daylight environment.

Color is a great way to give spaces in an open layout an identity, whether the home is a contemporary loft or a colonial with big rooms that flow together. Just as the layout plantings and flower beds defines outdoor garden "rooms," paint can set an open plan kitchen apart from its surroundings.

In this contemporary loft, opposite, curvy walls and citrus hues define the kitchen space. Bright colors emphasize its contours; furnishings, such as the upholstered stools, carry the loft's palette from room to room. Although orange is the major color in other rooms and hallways, it is an accent in the kitchen. Yellow-green walls in the cooking space augment the brightness and reflectivity of stainless steel appliances and fittings, and bright blue walls define its borders with other parts of the loft.

White Kitchens

THE HOME STAGE

White kitchens remain a popular choice for several reasons. In a room where good illumination is important, white reflects and amplifies available light from windows and fixtures. Many homeowners also appreciate the hygienic look of white; although this background makes dirt and stains highly visible, it also makes them easier to see and clean. On a positive note, the beautiful details of fine cabinetry, luxurious hardware, and attractive accessories stand out against a white background. And, like a monochromatic stage set in which the actors become the focal point, white creates a neutral canvas for the product—attractive and tasty meals—and the participants.

Tips for the All-White Kitchen

White walls and cabinets provide a backdrop for your accessories, so you can easily change the mood by making small changes in kitchen decor. In the summer, use blue or green to give the kitchen a cool look. Pick up this theme with linens, dishes, and a row of green herbs in blue pots along the windowsill.

When the seasons change, heat up the all-white look with accessories from the warmer side of the spectrum. Try red accessories at holiday time, yellow and orange in the fall.

To keep the pure look of squeaky-clean white, paint with durable, high-gloss finish, which is very easy to maintain. Or, if you prefer a matte look, use a clear coat of matte polyurethane over a low-gloss finish.

ABOVE Cabinets finished in creamy white enhance the period feel of this spacious, Victorian-style kitchen. Fine custom details, such as the beading around door and drawer openings, and exquisite polished hardware and fittings, stand out against the generous expanse of neutral painted background. White subway tiles used for the backsplash are an easy-care companion to the cabinets.

WHITE COTTAGE KITCHENS

In the long-ago days before custom-colored paint was sold in cans, homeowners made do with coatings made from local clays and pigments, ground up and mixed with water or other liquids so that they could be applied to a home's interior. Because lime and chalk are available nearly everywhere, the white and off-white coverings they produce are still used in homes around the world. And, because luxuries such as big windows and halogen lighting are still unavailable to many rural cottage-dwellers, the brightened interior produced by covering walls with white has remained for centuries a popular choice in many cultures.

For the homeowner with an authentic thatched cottage, or the contemporary householder who dreams of replicating a charming, country feeling in her kitchen, white walls are a wonderful starting point.

BELOW In this creamy-colored kitchen, an always-warm European cooker serves as the modern hearth for this country-style room. The owners' collection of copper pots and blue and white china become important decorative elements, distinctive against the neutral canvas of white walls and cupboards.

ABOVE In a cottage kitchen, even furnishings and accessories become part of the bright, all-white palette. White remains a popular choice for vacation houses; its clean, uncomplicated, and easy-to-care-for good looks reflect the calm, low-maintenance lifestyle that vacationers long to capture in their home away from home. Even decorating is simpler; a few, carefully edited color elements have greater impact in their cool white surroundings than they would in rooms with more complex color palettes.

REFINED SIMPLICITY

A simple plan, executed with high-quality elements and an uncomplicated palette, can convey elegance that many kitchens of double the size and budget cannot. In the white kitchen below, less becomes more in a carefully rendered layout that gives every form a function. The black dish racks, placed symmetrically at either side of the window, work in harmony with smooth bluestone counters and farmhouse sink. They provide a pleasant, crisp contrast with the white cabinets and walls. The homeowners' collection of white ironstone plays a dual role—as daily tableware and as decorative element in this straightforward but pleasing design.

Using open shelves and racks is an especially good idea for small kitchens; long runs of upper cabinets can create a closed-in feeling in a room that lacks a lot of floor space.

Open shelves that match or contrast with other kitchen elements are a decorative element as well as a storage solution.

BELOW Black–painted dishracks with white walls and lower cabinets accent the bluestone counter and sink.

What do you see? A wall niche, painted black to accentuate its geometry?
Or do you see what is, in fact, a wall cupboard with precise geometry that
adds contemporary punch to an all-white kitchen palette. The high contrast
between black and white creates an optical illusion and a sleek, modern
look. The simple, inexpensive construction of the wall cupboard above repays
its cost many times because it succeeds as a striking design element as well
as a functional space.

The Warm Hearth

The warmest portion of the spectrum—orange and red—is well known for its ability to energize the viewer and even stimulate the appetite. So it is not surprising that many homeowners enjoy being surrounded by these advancing colors in the kitchen. This room has become, for many, a hub of family activity, returning to its roots as the center of household life. A lively, energetic palette becomes a reflection of how people really use their kitchens, not only for food but also for fun.

Walls with a color wash that looks like terra-cotta create a vibrant background for the modern kitchen (opposite). The painted surfaces warm the layout of sleek wooden cabinets, contemporary hardware, and stainless steel appliances, making the space cheerful and inviting. And because of the cool accents— the silvery fittings, marble counters, and a dash of cool, bright blue for small storage drawers—the basic orange palette does not overheat the space.

Using the color-wash technique of brushing succeeding layers of related colors on the walls also mitigates the impact of bright orange. This application softens the walls' appearance, giving them a textured quality that mimics the surface of terra-cotta clay.

These walls would look at home in a Tuscan villa but also bring that same soft, rustic feel to a modern, urban dwelling.

THE NEW OLD KITCHEN

People who live in old houses love their rich patina, the marks that represent generations of homeowners who have inhabited these spaces. But each new family wants to put its stamp on a house, never more so than in the kitchen, which must change with new technologies and the replacement of old fittings that simply wear out.

This country kitchen, opposite, retains its beautiful and massive hand-hewn beams, and the owners have captured elements of its colonial character and coloring in the custom cabinetry and dramatic but traditional farmhouse sink and counters fabricated in soapstone. In the manner of old kitchen furniture, the new cabinets were hand-painted by professionals with an undercoating of pitch black milk paint. They were then overpainted with a coat of milk paint in barn red. This technique of using a dark base coat makes the top coat richer and deeper in tone. In times past, this house's earlier inhabitants might have used the same kind of milk paint with natural pigments made from iron oxide.

Tip

TOO BRIGHT? WHAT TO DO

Even when you test your color (see page 100), bright colors can turn out to be more intense than you planned. How can you tone it down? Sponging or color-washing a lighter or contrasting color over the bright layer definitely softens its visual impact.

The kitchen of an old Paris apartment, above, gets an injection of lively color with two tones of red. Candy pink walls, a red and white tiled backsplash, and a modern-era cabinet in a fresh coat of paint represent a low-cost strategy for refreshing a worn and tired space. The black and white checked flooring is a sophisticated complement to the room's new palette and 1950s-era style.

BRIGHT ACCENTS

Sometimes a stroke of bright color is all that is needed to punctuate a good kitchen design. Often filled with cabinets and appliances that capture most of the wall space, many kitchens have very little unused vertical surface. Therefore, using an accent of striking color along the soffits or the baseboards can act as a frame for the overall layout.

Cool whites and grays, brushed stainless steel, and polished hardwood floors give this contemporary kitchen, below, a sleek, professional look, tempered by strokes of orange paint on this room's limited stretches of bare wall. Looking through the open door, you can see the designer's strategy, carrying the theme set by the adjacent room's charcoal walls into the kitchen palette. The orange strokes define the kitchen space, setting it apart, yet the colors work beautifully next to one another.

Tips

RED AND ORANGE ACCENT IDEAS

Perking up a kitchen with warm shades of paint can enhance many design schemes. Red makes a great complement for many shades of green; likewise, orange is a perfect foil for blue. Paint these surfaces for accent:

• Wooden cabinet knobs; use a high-gloss paint for easy cleaning

• Baseboard or ceiling moldings, or the moldings around raised or recessed cabinet panels

• Shelf edges

• Cabinet interiors; this is an especially effective detail. A colorful cabinet interior can also make the contents of a cabinet easier to see.

Sunny Kitchens

Painting with yellow is like applying sunshine straight from the can. Light-starved rooms come alive when yellow is put to use in the decorating palette. The color of candlelight, spring daffodils, and all things golden, yellow makes a joyous statement in any room and will refresh the most timeworn kitchen.

The details of the beautiful wooden cabinetry in this Victorian-era home, opposite, would disappear if they were stained to mimic traditional dark walnut or mahogany. Even in minimal late-afternoon, light the woodwork has an inner glow; a golden shade of yellow reveals its intricate fretwork and moldings. Using related colors—yellow fits between green and red in the spectrum—for floors, door, and window trim creates a warm and harmonious setting for family gatherings and entertaining.

CHOOSING THE RIGHT YELLOW

Because yellow is the most reflective color in the spectrum, surfaces painted yellow tend to borrow from neighboring colors. This phenomenon can give yellow painted next to green a slightly greenish cast; then again, the golden yellow, right, looks pure and beautiful, in spite of the strong green used in the palette.

The best way to decide on a color is to test it. Even if you adore the palettes on these pages, give them a tryout before you paint.

Do not brush the color on the walls—yet. Buy some foam-core board at an office supply store, get a small can of each color you want to test, and paint one board each color. Prop the boards against the kitchen wall, furniture, or cabinets you want to paint. Look at the color in all kinds of light—daylight, lamplight, and whatever conditions exist in the room throughout the day. Place the board near a doorway to see how the color looks when moving into or out of the kitchen from adjacent rooms. Live with it for a few days. Then decide.

LIGHTEN UP

Kitchens with low levels of natural light can benefit from yellow's high
visibility quotient. It is the brightest natural hue in the spectrum, so dark
kitchens can instantly feel yellow's illuminating power.

The palette, right, shows how the application of yellow paint revives a space with few other cosmetic changes. Above, a kitchen with dated appliances gets a face-lift with an all-over coat of yellow. To provide contrast and interest, Mondrian-like blocks of red and black provide a contemporary touch to the traditional galley layout. Open shelves on the adjoining wall create an organized and attractive display of tableware and pottery, providing further dimension. A space that might otherwise feel dark and cheerless has become a bright spot for work and gathering.

In this kitchen, above, a 1960s-era dark-red brick wall absorbed the available window light and gave this otherwise neat and functional kitchen a dated appearance. But even with a tiny budget that precluded major changes, the space looks revitalized with the walls painted yellow and the cabinets, ceiling, and island finished with a light-reflecting white. Other inexpensive details—a valence over the kitchen window and a matching pillow on the yellow-cushioned bench—expand the color theme.

TWO-TONE YELLOW

The modern kitchen below has minimal details. Designed with plain cabinets and no visible hardware, the workspace is defined by an original color palette that sharply contrasts with the surrounding white environment. Two shades of yellow—a sunny hue for the cabinet fronts, and yellow-green for doors and drawers—provide a bright citrus palette. The use of two closely related colors is a subtle detail that makes the overall effect of the yellow kitchen more refined and sophisticated. Although either yellow, used alone, might seem garishly bright in the stark white surroundings, the two-toned treatment looks softer and more subdued. The addition of a warm, natural material, such as the wooden countertops, also mutes the brightness of this scheme.

When a kitchen has good bones, it seems quite wasteful to toss them in the landfill. Many 1950-era cabinets, made with solid wood and excellent craftsmanship, are worthy of restoration with a new paint job.

The light-filled kitchen, above, has a run of old cabinets made new by, above, yellow paint and replacement hardware. Instead of a single color, the home-owners have applied a second, golden shade of yellow in a diamond motif to all drawer and cabinet fronts, atop a coat of buttery yellow that also decks the walls. A new countertop and backsplash of white subway tiles complete the fresh, updated look.

The Colors of Nature

The natural world has always been an inspiring source of color ideas for a home's interior. The many blues of the sea and sky, the multiple greens in a spring field, even the neutral tones of a snowy landscape all serve as model palettes for manmade spaces. Browsing through the color chips at the local hardware or paint store, you can find repeated references to natural phenomena in the color names: forest green, Nantucket fog, Grecian wave, and on and on. Whole books have been written about natural color schemes for the home; this section is just a small sampling, using the dominant colors of the changing seasons as its kitchen palette theme.

AUTUMN

In early October, a breathtaking blend of reds, oranges, greens, and golds illuminates the forested hillsides in northern latitudes. The open-plan layout, left, reveals a kitchen and adjoining rooms that display the same fall colors, mixing harmoniously with warm, natural wood cabinets, moldings, and flooring. The homeowners selected low-sheen finishes, which mute the bright palette. To add shine, they have included shimmering metallic fixtures and cabinets, as well as polished countertops, creating a design with a pleasing balance of color and texture.

SELECTING A NATURAL PALETTE

One way to choose colors is to take a hike to your favorite spot in its best season, retrieving objects that appeal to you. Interesting stones, leaves, flowers, or bits of bark and branches can be the starting point for a palette that reflects your treasures in the natural world. (If your favorite spot is a park or other protected space, take photos—it is usually illegal to remove anything.)

WINTER

On close inspection, the winter landscape is anything but dull. Crevices in snow banks reveal sky blue shadows. Rough bark, examined carefully, is a symphony of grays, browns, and tans. Grasses in shades of umber and beige wave above the snow. The soft, subtle colors of winter can create a calming palette for the kitchen.

Pale gray, used for the kitchen cabinets and backsplash, above, couple with expansive views from the large windows to produce a peaceful space. Whereas some may use the kitchen as entertainment central, others seek out the daily round of preparing food and cleaning up as a respite from a hectic schedule and want surroundings that encourage quiet contemplation. The simple elegance of this palette make it a perfect environment for a working meditation.

EARLY SPRING

Nothing looks as fresh and green as the first signs of spring, poking up through the white dusting of a late snowstorm. The crocus and the snowdrop shoots are the color of hope.

The small, old-fashioned kitchen, right, has been likewise renewed with an application of these early spring colors; soft green walls and crisp, shiny white cabinets and trim make this room bright. The light palette also makes the small space more expansive. Green Depression glass tableware enhances the scheme, and because of its transparency, adds no bulk or clutter to the room.

Summer

Hold a variegated bouquet of flowers in your hand, and you will see a riot of color against a green background. This simple exercise demonstrates how green acts as a neutral backdrop for most other colors, blending many hues together in harmony. Foliage is the base for most garden plans, and green is a wonderful background in a colorful kitchen.

Because of its association with everything that grows, green is a natural choice for a summer-inspired palette. Depending on your own bright favorites, you can select many combinations that will work well with a chosen shade of green.

In the 1950-era kitchen, opposite, the highly functional original layout is preserved, and the cabinets have been painted with a shade evocative of the Art Deco era—a time when pastels prevailed in the popular palette. The homeowners have chosen a sparkling violet hue for the counters and backsplash, another summer garden color that lends its brightness to this happy kitchen scheme. An eclectic assortment of pottery, small appliances, and other collectibles in a rainbow of colors decorates this kitchen like a border of summer blooms on the garden path.

Other Summer Palettes

To evoke the feeling of summer, the colors of surf, sand, and sky can also create the carefree aura of the summer months. Pale blue and tan might remind you of the beach; a rainbow of pastels mimics a summer sunset. Lighter tints will best duplicate the long, bright days of July and August.

High Contrast

Working with black, white, and neutral colors—grays, tans, beiges—creates kitchen spaces more defined by volume, dimension, and texture than by their brilliant hues. Using these non-colors, as they are sometimes called, directs the eye to shape, form, and finish details. This section provides four different approaches to using light and dark neutrals together for dramatic kitchen palettes.

Even with such rustic details as hand-hewn ceiling beams and a built-in, wood-fired pizza oven, this kitchen, above, has dramatic, contemporary flair. Its simple palette—white, beige, and black, with stainless steel fixtures and appliances as silvery accents—brings into focus the unique structural elements of the design.

The hood over the cooking island has the texture and mass of an adobe hearth, becoming the room's focal point. The lower cabinets and refrigerator are black, so their forms recede, creating a background for all the interesting, light-colored shapes in the foreground.

Which came first: the dark chocolate-brown paint on the vintage metal cabinets or the striking still-life painting over the sink? No matter which element inspired the kitchen palette below, deep, dark brown is an original and exciting counterpoint to white. It adds a touch of glamour to this simple but sleek design.

When a sink is located without a window above it, the design problem of what to put in place of a view can be handled in a variety of ways. Often, a mirror allows someone at the sink to watch the goings-on in other parts of the kitchen. If the sink wall opens to the dining area, a cutout pass-through can connect the cook to family and guests. In this case, a single, beautiful piece of art creates a focal point for the space.

EVENING DRAMA

No longer hidden behind closed doors, the kitchen is nearly everyone's favorite place to gather. Many homeowners lavish attention and luxury materials on its design, making the kitchen not only functional but gorgeous as well.

Using painted effects to mimic expensive materials is one way to get the deluxe look without the hefty price tag. In this kitchen, opposite, the walls and ceiling have been painted to imitate marble in a beautiful combination of tans and beiges. Jet-black cabinets create a dramatic contrast, and soft, dimmable hanging lights above the counter provide an intimate dining space. The design looks rich.

Many homeowners worry that a dark, dark palette will make their spaces look like black voids. But even a kitchen where black predominates need not resemble a cave. In this kitchen, below, a large European range and its backsplash are brightened by the accents of stainless steel and a short run of white cabinets. This is a no-nonsense setting, designed for serious cooks, but the contrast in materials makes the kitchen look hardworking but not cold.

Of course, excellent ambient and task lighting are essential in any workspace where dark colors rule. Reflective materials, such as stainless steel appliance fronts, also reflect and amplify existing light.

Resources

COLOR HELP

The color wheel is a great visual resource for determining how to combine colors in a room. The Color Wheel Company sells a variety of wheels, including an Interior Design Wheel, which demonstrate hundreds of possible combinations. www.colorwheelco.com, 541-929-7526.

Several manufacturers offer small paint samples that you can test on a board without buying a large quantity of paint. Devine Paint (www.devinecolor.com), Farrow & Ball (www.farrow-ball.com), Fine Paints of Europe (www.fine-paints.com), all offer sample sizes of their premium paints.

MORE PAINT INFORMATION

Want more painting pointers? Contact the Paint Quality Institute (www.paintquality.com) for plenty of facts and tips.

The National Paint and Coatings Association (NPCA) offers extensive information about choosing paint colors on its website (www.paintinfo.org).

Looking for professional help for your paint job? The Paint and Decorating Contractors of America (PDCA) is a venerable organization to which more than 3,000 painting companies belong. Their website provides helpful hints about hiring a pro, plus a convenient 800 number to find local, trained, and licensed painting contractors in your area. Visit the PDCA website at www.pdca.org and click on "consumer information."

A Field Guide for Painting, Home Maintenance, and Renovation Work. This booklet can be ordered from the National Lead Information Center at 800-424-5323 or downloaded from www.hud.gov/offices/lead.

National Institute for Occupational Safety www.cdc.gov.niosh/homepage.html

Mine Safety and Health Administration www.msha.gov/

PAINT COMPANIES

Benjamin Moore
51 Chestnut Ridge Road
Montvale, NJ 07645
800-344-0400
www.benjaminmoore.com

C2 Paints
www.c2color.com
(Product information and retail locations)

California Paints
169 Waverly Street
Cambridge, MA 02139-0007
800-225-1141
www.californiapaints.com

Farrow & Ball
1054 Yonge Street
Toronto Ontario
Canada
877-363-1040
farrowball@bellnet.ca

Farrow & Ball Limited
Uddens Estate
WIMBORNE
Dorset BH21 7NL
United Kingdom
01202-876141
info@farrow-ball.com

Farrow & Ball Inc
845-369-4912
usasales@farrow-ball.com

Glidden
ICI Paints
Cleveland, OH 44115
800-GLIDDEN
www.glidden.com

McCloskey Faux and Wood Finishes
1191 Wheeling Road
Wheeling, IL 60090
800-345-4530
techsupport@valspar.com

Pittsburgh Paints
PPG Industries, Inc.
One PPG Place
Pittsburgh, PA 15272
800-441-9695
www.ppgaf.com

Pratt and Lambert
(The Sherwin-Williams Co.)
800-BUYPRAT
www.prattandlambert.com

Ralph Lauren Paint
ICI Paints
Cleveland, OH 44115
800-379-POLO
www.rlhome.polo.com

Sherwin-Williams Company
101 Prospect Avenue
Cleveland, OH 44115
216-566-2000
www.sherwin-williams.com

Valspar Consumer Products
Customer Service
1191 Wheeling Road
Wheeling, IL 60090
800-845-9061
techsupport@valspar.com

TOOLS AND SUPPLIES

Bestt Liebco Corporation
1201 Jackson Street
Philadelphia, PA 19148
800-523-9095
customerservice@besttcorp.com
www.besttliebco.com

Charles Street Supply
54 Charles Street
Boston, MA 02114
617-367-9046
online@charlesstsupply.com
(*Plaster washers*)

Corona Brushes, Inc.
5065 Savarese Circle
Tampa, FL 33634
800-458-3483
www.coronabrushes.com

DAP Products, Inc.
2400 Boston Street
Suite 200
Baltimore, MD 21224
410-675-2100
www.dap.com
(*Caulking, fillers, spackle*)

Easy Mask/Loparex
7700 Griffin Way
Willowbrook, IL 60527
800-634-1303
www.easymask.com
(*Masking papers, plastics, tape*)

The Flood Company
P.O. Box 2535
Hudson, OH 44236-0035
800-321-3444
www.floodco.com
(*Paint additives*)

Goldblatt
Stanley Tools Group
480 Myrtle Street
New Britain, CT 06053
www.stanleyworks.com
(*Drywall, plaster, tools*)

Hyde Manufacturing Company
54 Eastford Road
Southbridge, MA 01550
800-872-4933
info@hydetools.com

Marshalltown Tools
104 South 8th Avenue
Marshalltown, IA 50158
641-753-5999
www.marshalltown.com

Norton Abrasives
Gainsville, GA 30501
770-967-3954
www.nortonabrasives.com
(*Sandpaper*)

Purdy Brushes
13201 North Lombard
Portland, OR 97203-6410
503-286-8217
info@purdycorp.com

Red Devil
2400 Vauxhall Road
Union, NJ 07083
800-4-A-Devil
www.reddevil.com
(*Tools, caulking, spackle*)

Shur-line
4051 S. Iowa Avenue
St. Francis, WI 53235
877-Shurline
www.shurline.com
(*Paint pads, tools*)

USG (United States Gypsum)
125 South Franklin
Chicago, IL 60606-4678
800-874-4968
usg4you@usg.com

Warner Manufacturing Company
13435 Industrial Park Blvd.
Minneapolis, MN 55441
877-WARNER-8
www.warnertool.com

The Wooster Brush Company
604 Madison Avenue
P.O. Box 6010
Wooster, OH 44691-6010
800-382-7246
www.woosterbrush.com

Zinsser Co. Inc.
173 Belmont Drive
Somerset, NJ 08875
732-469-8100
www.zinsser.com
(*The PAPERTIGER®*)

HANDCRAFTED CABINETS

Crown Point Cabinetry
153 Charlestown Road
Claremont, NH 03743
800-999-4994
www.crown-point.com

Photographer Credits

Todd Caverly, Brian Vanden Brink Photos, 33

Courtesy of Crown Point Cabinetry/www.crown-point.com, 6; 72-73; 88-89; 97

Elizabeth Felicella/Leven Betts Studio, 79

Elizabeth Felicella/Ghislaine Viñas, Design, 56; 99

Tria Giovan, 13; 63; 65; 107; 110-111; 113

Courtesy of Glidden, an ICI Paint Brand/www.glidden.com, 2; 5; 7; 10; 11; 12; 15; (right); 17; 20; 22; 23; 24; 28; 36; 38; 45; 47; 54 (bottom); 82, (Glidden paint colors: Sun Rays, Pure White, Huckleberry, Rapture); 84, (Glidden paint colors: Rapture, Huckleberry, Sun Rays, Champagne Sparkle, Black, Limelight); 92, (Glidden paint colors: Pure Black, European White); 93, (Glidden paint colors: Black, Pure White); 101, (Glidden paint colors: Gold Sunset, Sun God, Forest Green, Rapture, Black, Pure White); 104-105, (Glidden paint colors: Pure White, Celestial Sun); 117, (Glidden paint colors: Crisp Linen, Stewart House Brown, Fencepost); 122; 124; 127

Steve Gross & Susan Daley, 32; 67

Steve Gross & Susan Daley/Janna Ritz Design, 61; 114

Steve Gross & Susan Daley/V. & J. Tozzi, Design, 64; 81

Lisa Jordan, 48; 59

Ray Main/Mainstream/Flying Duck Enterprises, 102-103

Ray Main/Mainstream/Plain & Simple Kitchens, 76

Rob Melnychuk, 9; 119

Shelley Metcalf, 116

Red Cover/Tim Evan-Cook, 98

Red Cover/Jake Fitzjones, 15 (left); 30

Red Cover/Brian Harrison, 87

Red Cover/Home Base, 94

Red Cover/Henry Wilson, 106

Eric Roth, 26-27; 75; 90; 120

Eric Roth/Susan Sargent Designs, 52-53; 71

Eric Roth/Astrid Vigeland, Stylist, 91

Brian Vanden Brink/Stephen Blatt, Architect, 108

Brian Vanden Brink/Elliott, Elliott, Norelius Architecture, 42

Brian Vanden Brink/ Mark Hutker & Associates Architects, Inc., 8; 19

Brian Vanden Brink/Dominic Merca Dante, Architect, 62

Brian Vanden Brink/Jack Silverio, 29

Brian Vanden Brink/Rob Whitten, Architect, 51

About the Authors

Steve Jordan is an architectural conservator, preservation specialist, and writer. He is author of *Rehab Rochester: A Sensible Guide for Old-House Maintenance, Repair, and Rehabilitation* (Landmark Society of Western New York, 1995), and has written numerous articles for magazines and professional journals. He has been a contributing editor for *Old-House Journal* since 1998 and frequently gives lectures and workshops on historic paint finishes and other topics related to home maintenance, preservation, and repair. He lives in Rochester, New York.

Judy Ostrow is an independent journalist who specializes in color, architecture, and interior design. She is author of *Painting Rooms* (Rockport Publishers, 2001). Her articles appear in national magazines, including *Home, Natural Home, This Old House, House Beautiful*, and *Woman's Day.* She lives in Westchester County, New York.

Acknowledgments

I would like to acknowledge Gordon Bock, editor of *Old-House Journal,*
for recommending me for this book. I also thank Betsy Gammons and Mary
Ann Hall for their patience and hard work. Most of all, I thank my wife,
Lisa, and my children, Wilkes and Pierce, for allowing me to disappear at
the computer for long periods of time without being disturbed. –Steve Jordan

My thanks to Betsy Gammons, Rockport's intrepid photo editor, who had an
answer to every question and a solution to every problem. I also appreciate
the efforts of all who make beautiful, colorful kitchens: the designers, the
contractors, the suppliers, and the homeowners who allow us to view, enjoy,
and learn from the final product. –Judy Ostrow